A YEAR OF CREATIVE WRITING PROMPTS

LOVE IN INK

Copyright © 2019 Love in Ink.
All rights reserved.

ISBN-13: 978-1517402969
ISBN-10: 1517402964

INDEX

INTRODUCTION II
BOOK GUIDE III
DAILY PROMPTS 1
MORNING FIVES 225
PROMPTS BY GENRE 232
    ACTION/ADVENTURE 232
    FANTASY/SCI-FI 237
    GENERAL 253
    HORROR 270
    HUMOR/MAGICAL REALISM 275
    JOURNALING 295
    MYSTERY/THRILLER 301
    ROMANCE/RELATIONSHIPS 315
    WRITING CHALLENGES 325
THANK YOU! 349

INTRODUCTION

Writing is a fickle Muse. There are days when a writer's head is filled to the brim with color, with words, with sounds and faces and ideas that beg to be put down on paper, to be made real. And then there are those days - most days - when nothing, not even a drop of imagination, can be squeezed forth from the quill of a writer's mind.

The *Love in Ink* team is composed of two dedicated, passionate, sleep-deprived writers. We have experienced the woes of writer's block first-hand, and have found the solution simpler than we could have ever expected: Writing prompts! A fresh idea, an interesting line, even a curious word is at times enough to kick a writer's imagination back into gear.

This book contains our very own, very best writing prompts - three a day, every day, for a whole year! Inside, you will find everything from writing challenges to solid book ideas, to exercises aimed toward making you a better writer. You will never be bored - or stumped for an idea - again!

BOOK GUIDE

This book is styled as advertised: Three-prompts-per-day, every day, for a whole year. Accordingly, you will find the writing prompts randomized across genres and grouped in threes over 366 days (we made it a leap year ☺).

If you find yourself wanting to practice a single genre, simply turn to the **"Prompts by Genre"** section of this book. There, you will find all writing prompts grouped by genre. For your convenience, we have included checkable boxes next to each prompt. This way, you can keep track of the ones you have already filled.

As writers, we have found a minimalist style of presentation the most pleasing to the eye and mind. Therefore, we have styled this book so it contains one to two days of prompts per page. We hope that this will allow you to focus completely on the prompt before you, shut off your surroundings, and do what you love most - write.

Happy writing! ~*The Love in Ink Team*

DAILY PROMPTS

Welcome to your first daily prompts sequence! Below, you will find the prompts, plus an explanation of how the prompts are structured. If you would rather have the complete list of prompts, you will find it under "Prompts by Genre" beginning on page 232. Enjoy!

Day 1

Five-minute prompt:

> **The five-minute prompt is composed of a single word. It is meant to get your imagination running - don't over think it! Read the word, then write what comes to mind. Don't edit, don't worry about it being chaotic or incoherent - just write!**

- [ ] Peaches

- ***Midday prompt:***

    A prompt in a random genre. Could be anything from a topic for a journal entry to high-paced action.

- Write from the perspective of a mouse in a cupboard.

Dinner prompt:

   Same as the Midday Prompt; a prompt in a random genre. Could be anything from a topic for a journal entry to high-paced action.

- A star falls in a family's backyard. Only it's not a star but a very friendly alien.

Day 2
Five-minute prompt:
- [ ] Thunder

Midday prompt:
- [ ] Your pet dragon is misbehaving.

Dinner prompt:
- [ ] The shadows on your wall are speaking. Write about the conversation that follows.

Day 3
Five-minute prompt:
- [ ] Circlet

Midday prompt:
- [ ] A magical mishap shrinks your character for twenty four hours. How does the day go?

Dinner prompt:
- [ ] A girl grows wings. Nothing else about her changes, and no explanation seems forthcoming about where the wings came from. What is more, they seem to have a mind of their own...

Day 4
Five-minute prompt:
- [ ] Earl

Midday prompt:
- [ ] Write a WANTED ad for a serial cat burglar who is, in fact, a cat.

Dinner prompt:
- [ ] Your character has been turned into a magical creature. What kind of creature is it? How does their day go?

Day 5
Five-minute prompt:
- [ ] Smudged

Midday prompt:
- [ ] Describe your morning routine using the most eccentric words and phrases that come to mind.

Dinner prompt:
- [ ] Have you had a reoccurring dream? What was it about? Write a short story around it.

Day 6
Five-minute prompt:
- ☐ Ash

Midday prompt:
- ☐ Create a holiday! Describe its history, how to celebrate it, etc. Word it as an essay about the holiday - as if completing a boring school assignment.

Dinner prompt:
- ☐ Let's banish some monsters! Write a funny story featuring your biggest fear.

Day 7
Five-minute prompt:
- ☐ Fall

Midday prompt:
- ☐ Personify an object around you. Your teacup for example. What does it do and say?

Dinner prompt:
- ☐ Write a one-scene play about a Princess who has been turned into a Prince.

Day 8

Five-minute prompt:
☐ Sear

Midday prompt:
☐ Write an origin story for the Easter Bunny.

Dinner prompt:
☐ Describe a place you find beautiful and calming. It can be imaginary or real.

Day 9

Five-minute prompt:
☐ Grasp

Midday prompt:
☐ What did you have for lunch? Describe it as if you are in a commercial selling that particular food.

Dinner prompt:
☐ Create a deity. Describe its origin, its powers, how it looks - anything you want.

Day 10
Five-minute prompt:
- [ ] Seep

Midday prompt:
- [ ] Write a short story featuring a minor character from one of your larger works - someone you never had a reason or occasion to flesh out. Make the story about them!

Dinner prompt:
- [ ] Create a creature. Describe how it looks, where it lives, what it eats, its behavior.

Day 11
Five-minute prompt:
- [ ] Fair

Midday prompt:
- [ ] Pick a celebrity and feature them as a character in a story - folktale, myth, whatever you like.

Dinner prompt:
- [ ] Write about a trip you have taken. If you have ever traveled outside your native country, write about that journey: What stuck with you?

Day 12

Five-minute prompt:
- ☐ Amber

Midday prompt:
- ☐ Write about a goose whose best friend is a cat.

Dinner prompt:
- ☐ Pick a word/phrase in a foreign language (at random, if you can!) and use it in a story.
Need some help? Here is a list of ten random foreign words:
  - **朝 (Asa)** - Morning
  - **До свидания (Dosvi'dania)** - Goodbye
  - **(der) Schatten** - (the) Shadow
  - **ανατολή ηλίου (anatolíilíou)** - Sunrise
  - **Tiarna** - Lord
  - **Guanti** - Gloves
  - **Grasker** - Pumpkin
  - **내기 (Naegi)** - Miser
  - **Õhtu** - Night, evening
  - **Anioł** - Angel

Day 13

Five-minute prompt:
- ☐ Salt

Midday prompt:
- ☐ Write about a world that has no colors in it.

Dinner prompt:
- ☐ Set a story in a mythical location, either fictional or historical.

   In need of inspiration? Here is a list of ten places of myths, both fictional and not.

- **Alexandria**: City named after Alexander the Great. It was host to a tremendous library (Library of Alexandria) and served as a center of knowledge. The Library's eventual destruction resulted in an immense loss of knowledge still mourned today.
- **Babylon**: A historically important city in ancient Mesopotamia. Known for the wonder of the Hanging Gardens, as well as a setting to a number of Biblical (the Tower of Bibel) and Mesopotamian myths.
- **Elysian Fields**: A mythological realm of final rest for fallen warriors and worthy souls in Greek mythology.
- **Kyöpelinvuori**: A fictional place in the mountains in Finnish mythology. Said to be haunted by dead women.

- **Lemuria**: An ancient land rumored to have been the home of an extremely advanced civilization. Thought to have sunk in the wake of a natural disaster. Thought to have existed between the Indian and Pacific Oceans.
- **Muspelheim**: A realm of fire in Norse mythology.
- **Shambhala**: According to Tibetan Buddhist mythology: An ancient kingdom hidden in the Himalayas, ruled by the governing deity of our world.
- **Troy**: A city in Greek mythology that was besieged and eventually overran by Greek armies. Thought to have been located on the shores of present-day Israel.
- **Valhalla**: In Norse mythology, Valhalla is a majestic hall in which Odin rules over all worlds.

Day 14
Five-minute prompt:
- ☐ Dimple

Midday prompt:
- ☐ Create and describe an alien planet capable of sustaining life. How closely do you imagine it would resemble ours? What kind of life would it bear?

Dinner prompt:
- ☐ Make up a fairy tale. Make sure it has all the fairy tale elements (the adage in particular), but otherwise write as you will!

Day 15
Five-minute prompt:
- ☐ Grain

Midday prompt:
- ☐ A character finds a magical turtle. It follows him/her around and tries to "help" by making small wishes the character utters aloud come true. The results are more embarrassing than anything else.

Dinner prompt:
- ☐ A character you have created comes to life. Congrats - you've got a new roommate!

Day 16
Five-minute prompt:
- [ ] Knot

Midday prompt:
- [ ] A woman receives a gift from a secret admirer. It arrives in a small crate that is cold to the touch. The accompanying note states that her admirer wishes he could touch her heart with his words.

  What is in the crate? How does the woman react?

Dinner prompt:
- [ ] A surly teenager wakes up in one of the Grimm Brother's more morbid fairy tales: Bluebeard.

Day 17
Five-minute prompt:
- [ ] Hour

Midday prompt:
- [ ] Describe a tree in full bloom. Try not to use cliché phrases.

Dinner prompt:
- [ ] Write a prayer. The tone does not need to be religious. Try for a simple, honest wording.

Day 18
Five-minute prompt:
- [ ] Callous

Midday prompt:
- [ ] Make up a word. Give the definition and use it in a sentence.

Dinner prompt:
- [ ] A love confession letter gets delivered to the wrong address. The sender realizes what has happened and tries to get it back. What happens?

Day 19
Five-minute prompt:
- [ ] Crumpled

Midday prompt:
- [ ] An ordinary, boring man gains a superpower. What kind of power is it? What does he do with it?

Dinner prompt:
- [ ] Write a short story from the perspective of a fairy-tale villain. For example, the witch from *Hansel and Gretel*, or the Queen from *Snow White*.

Day 20
Five-minute prompt:
- [ ] Tiara

Midday prompt:
- [ ] Write about a lawyer who lives in a city at the bottom of the sea.

Dinner prompt:
- [ ] Pick a scene from a movie you like. Now rewrite that scene as a parody.

Day 21
Five-minute prompt:
- [ ] Tumble

Midday prompt:
- [ ] An elderly woman is gardening when she discovers what appears to be a treasure map buried in her back yard. It seems to lead to a spot on the outskirts of town. What does she find where X marks the spot?

Dinner prompt:
- [ ] A young man is in a minor accident. When he wakes up in the hospital following the incident, he sees a strange being sitting by his bed. Who/what is it? What happens?

Day 22
Five-minute prompt:
☐ Arrow

Midday prompt:
☐ A renowned secret agent is tasked with stealing an important document from the home of a Mafia Don. During the operation, he runs into another man set on the very same document – a thief with a flamboyant personality and a flair for the dramatic that grates on the agent's nerves. When the two men are discovered by the Don's security, they have to work together in order to avoid being captured.

Write a short story around the mission and its outcome.

Dinner prompt:
☐ An old man sits in a garden, alone. Describe his thoughts and surroundings. Try to create a specific mood with your description.

Day 23
Five-minute prompt:
- ☐ Spill

Midday prompt:
- ☐ An artist is harangued by a woman who wants to buy one of his portraits. Write their conversation. Try to make the story dialogue-only and still convey its plot and characters.

Dinner prompt:
- ☐ Write a story featuring a character that is completely clueless about what is happening around them. Recommended genre: Humor.

Day 24
Five-minute prompt:
- ☐ Bone

Midday prompt:
- ☐ A little girl hears a strange noise coming from a dried-up well. She stands on her tippy-toes and peers over the well's rim, and sees…

Dinner prompt:
- ☐ A teenager is visiting his grandmother in her small hometown village. Describe a day they spend together.

Day 25
Five-minute prompt:
- [ ] Bullet

Midday prompt:
- [ ] A couple bickers over something stupid. The two give each other the silent treatment, then make up. Write the scene.

Dinner prompt:
- [ ] A fox transforms into a human for a day. Write what follows.

Day 26
Five-minute prompt:
- [ ] Bite

Midday prompt:
- [ ] A dim-witted knight decides to take on a fire-breathing dragon in order to save a lovely princess. The dragon is more amused than anything else.

Dinner prompt:
- [ ] Write a story featuring one of your ancestors.

Day 27
Five-minute prompt:
- [ ] Flesh

Midday prompt:
- [ ] An angel and a demon are trapped in a single mortal body after a supernatural mishap. What happens?

Dinner prompt:
- [ ] A strange girl is riding the train late at night. A man approaches her.

Day 28
Five-minute prompt:
- [ ] Full

Midday prompt:
- [ ] Two men are vying for the attention of a woman. What does each offer? How do they approach her? Who – if either – does she choose in the end?

Dinner prompt:
- [ ] A stressed-out businessman is turned into a cat by one of his clients.

Day 29
Five-minute prompt:
- Moonrise

Midday prompt:
- A girl sits on a bridge, singing. She seems sad. Who is she? Write a story about her.

Dinner prompt:
- Write a conversation between a dragon and the princess it has captured.

Day 30
Five-minute prompt:
- Legion

Midday prompt:
- A man sees a boy snatch a woman's handbag. He chases after the thief and is able to catch up to him - only to find out that the boy is his son.

Dinner prompt:
- A bear moves into a new apartment building and goes to introduce him/herself to the neighbors.

Day 31
Five-minute prompt:
- Asunder

Midday prompt:
- A teenage boy helps his aged neighbor clean her house as she prepares to move out. Touched, the woman tells him that he is welcome to anything he finds in the attic. What does the boy find?

Dinner prompt:
- Describe a rainy evening in a busy city.

Day 32
Five-minute prompt:
- Caravan

Midday prompt:
- Your mobile is judging your text messages.

Dinner prompt:
- A man works for a delivery service in a remote, mountainous area. One morning, he receives a suspicious-looking crate to deliver to a local farm.

Day 33
Five-minute prompt:
☐ Myth

Midday prompt:
☐ A woman receives a strange phone call. The caller's voice is muffled and somewhat difficult to understand. What does the caller want? What does your character do?

Dinner prompt:
☐ Two friends lose their way in the mountains while hiking. Thankfully, they are able to find an empty cabin before night sets around them. It is well-stocked, the heat is running, and all electronics – except the phone lines – seem in check. As the night progresses, however, strange things start to happen…

Day 34
Five-minute prompt:
- ☐ Beast

Midday prompt:
- ☐ Write the world's most dreadfully clichéd poem.

Dinner prompt:
- ☐ Retell a folktale. Try to include as many different points of view as there are characters in it.

  In need of inspiration? Try one the following tales:
  - Red Riding Hood
  - Hensel and Gretel
  - The Big Bad Wolf and the Three Piglets

Day 35
Five-minute prompt:
- ☐ Tart

Midday prompt:
- ☐ Describe a humorously terrible day of family fun at the beach.

Dinner prompt:
- ☐ A brattish Prince runs away from home. He meets a bored bandit at a small, crowded tavern. What happens?

Day 36
Five-minute prompt:
☐ Treacherous

Midday prompt:
☐ A shy florist falls in love with the owner of the small bakery next door. Unable to say what he feels, he tries to show his feelings through the language of flowers. Unfortunately, his one true love cannot tell a weed from a peony...

Dinner prompt:
☐ A man gains the ability to speak with inanimate objects. Describe his first day at work following the strange occurrence.

Day 37
Five-minute prompt:
☐ Ravine

Midday prompt:
☐ A teacher finds a letter written by one of the worst troublemakers in her class. The letter is addressed to the boy's mother, and seems to have been discarded, unsent. What is in the letter?

Dinner prompt:
☐ Two cockroaches, talking about life.

Day 38
Five-minute prompt:
- Shadow

Midday prompt:
- A little girl brings her pet demon to show-and-tell at school.

Dinner prompt:
- A little boy tells his imaginary friend what he wants to be when he grows up.

Day 39
Five-minute prompt:
- Stilted

Midday prompt:
- Two travelers sit beneath a large, old tree and talk about the places they have seen during their wanderings.

Dinner prompt:
- The tree from the previous prompt grumbles about humans while it listens to the travelers' conversation.

Day 40
Five-minute prompt:
- ☐ Silhouette

Midday prompt:
- ☐ A bunny and a Doberman play together.

Dinner prompt:
- ☐ A girl chases after baby ducks in her grandmother's backyard.

Day 41
Five-minute prompt:
- ☐ Facade

Midday prompt:
- ☐ A mermaid gossiping with a cat.

Dinner prompt:
- ☐ A girl protects her little sister from bullies.

Day 42
Five-minute prompt:
- ☐ Fruit

Midday prompt:
- ☐ Two skunks take a walk around their neighborhood.

Dinner prompt:
- ☐ A geneticist successfully creates a talking dog. Now, if he could only get the stupid thing to shut up...

Day 43
Five-minute prompt:
- ☐ Sin

Midday prompt:
- ☐ A young girl gets lost while camping with her class. She stumbles upon a strange hut in the forest...

Dinner prompt:
- ☐ A boy gets sucked into his favorite video game. Write a short scene around a single level of that game.

Day 44
Five-minute prompt:
- ☐ Garden

Midday prompt:
- ☐ Make yourself a cup of coffee or tea. Now, foretell your own future by reading the patterns in the liquid.

Dinner prompt:
- ☐ A scientist observing a meteor shower sees something other than stars falling to Earth...

Day 45
Five-minute prompt:
- ☐ Crown

Midday prompt:
- ☐ A toddler draws something strange during playtime at school.

Dinner prompt:
- ☐ Dionysos, the Greek god of wine and revelry, takes a mortal form in order to visit the human world. Only he might've been one goblet too many into his wine while he was performing the enchantments that turned him into a human. He is now stuck in the body of an elderly woman in downtown New York.

Day 46

Five-minute prompt:
- [ ] Rose

Midday prompt:
- [ ] A pirate captures the son of a corrupt British noble and blackmails the man for ransom. While the boy's father is properly cowed, the boy is more excited than scared by his being kidnapped by pirates.

Dinner prompt:
- [ ] A writer meets a mysterious woman in a bar. He feels drawn to her; what is more, she seems strangely familiar...

Day 47

Five-minute prompt:
- [ ] Thorn

Midday prompt:
- [ ] Pick a name, at random. Research its history and write a short summary of its roots.

Dinner prompt:
- [ ] Write a short story containing an incredible amount of adjectives. Seriously, go wild.

Day 48

Five-minute prompt:

☐ Kiss

Midday prompt:

☐ A dark night in a foreign city. A tourist is walking along the banks of a river, on her way back to her hotel. Suddenly, a shadow shifts to her right. She turns-

Dinner prompt:

☐ A demon takes a human form in order to trick a pious mortal into giving away their soul. Only, the mortal in question is not so easily duped: He/she sees through the demon's disguise and baits the demon right back.

Day 49

Five-minute prompt:

☐ Forsaken

Midday prompt:

☐ Three friends pool their money together and buy a whole bunch of lottery tickets. One of the tickets ends up winning half a million dollars! What do they do with the money?

Dinner prompt:

☐ Two strangers meet on a dark road in the middle of a forest. One has a secret; the other is running from something.

Day 50
Five-minute prompt:
- ☐ Verbose

Midday prompt:
- ☐ A young mother saying goodbye to her child on his/her first day at school.

Dinner prompt:
- ☐ A woman is invited to the engagement party of a friend who, years earlier, got her fired in order to take her job. The friend does not know that the woman is aware of his/her betrayal.

Day 51
Five-minute prompt:
- ☐ Guilt

Midday prompt:
- ☐ Dark skies, empty world.

Dinner prompt:
- ☐ A chase that spans continents, between two people who profess to hate each other, but cannot quite let go.

Day 52
Five-minute prompt:
- Golden

Midday prompt:
- Write of a world in which wishes come true - if one is willing to pay their price.

Dinner prompt:
- Two musicians from competing bands fall in love. Each dedicates a song to the other. Their bandmates are not amused.

Day 53
Five-minute prompt:
- Rouge

Midday prompt:
- An old woman discovers the fountain of youth. If she drinks from its waters, she will be young and beautiful again - but will also forget everything she has ever experienced. What does she do?

Dinner prompt:
- Describe the following words in the most unique way possible:
Love, Desire, Grief

Day 54
Five-minute prompt:
- [ ] Rogue

Midday prompt:
- [ ] A man is driving towards work, in heavy traffic. Suddenly, the car next to his disappears. So does the one in front of him, the one behind him...until he is quite alone on the road.

Dinner prompt:
- [ ] Misadventures in cooking. Pasta on the ceiling, fire in the oven - that sort of thing.

Day 55
Five-minute prompt:
- [ ] Stone

Midday prompt:
- [ ] A baby duck imprints on a lawyer, and follows him wherever he goes. Including the courtroom.

Dinner prompt:
- [ ] A man finds a strange ring in his wife's purse.

Day 56
Five-minute prompt:
- Fire

Midday prompt:
- An unlikely romance.

Dinner prompt:
- Two friends are on a road trip when they are caught in a terrible storm. Their car is wrecked, their phones are out of service...and they seem to have ended up somewhere strange indeed.

Day 57
Five-minute prompt:
- Crystal

Midday prompt:
- Write a story around a recipe.

Dinner prompt:
- A historical figure is resurrected, and sent to spend a single day at a modern-day high school/college. What do they think? Need inspiration? Resurrect:
    - Julius Caesar
    - Cleopatra
    - Vladimir Lenin
    - Aristotle
    - Friedrich Nietzsche

Day 58
Five-minute prompt:
- [ ] Silence

Midday prompt:
- [ ] A man purchases a strange pet in a mysterious pet store.

Dinner prompt:
- [ ] A boy buys a gift for his mother.

Day 59
Five-minute prompt:
- [ ] Echo

Midday prompt:
- [ ] Three siblings reunite after the death of their father.

Dinner prompt:
- [ ] Write about something that has happened to you. Style the essay as a newspaper report.

Day 60
Five-minute prompt:
- [ ] Iris

Midday prompt:
- [ ] A warrior returns home after a terrible war.

Dinner prompt:
- [ ] Write a short story featuring a British sailor exploring the oceans in the 1800s.

Day 61
Five-minute prompt:
- [ ] Ego

Midday prompt:
- [ ] Set a story in a historic era of your choice. Need inspiration? Try:
    - Ancient Egypt
    - Heian Period Japan
    - Germany, in the years leading up to the Second World War
    - Tsarist Russia, right before the Bolshevik Revolution

Dinner prompt:
- [ ] A girl has reoccurring dreams about a kind boy with a bright smile. Years later, she meets a man who reminds her of that boy...

Day 62
Five-minute prompt:
- ☐ Goddess

Midday prompt:
- ☐ Write about a tragedy that does not feature death or blood: A simple, everyday heartbreak.

Dinner prompt:
- ☐ A newly-retired army Colonel visits someone he once loved dearly, but had to disregard in order to fulfill his duty to his country.

Day 63
Five-minute prompt:
- ☐ Owl

Midday prompt:
- ☐ A mysterious store sells strange perfumes.

Dinner prompt:
- ☐ A happy puppy playing with its favorite human.

Day 64

Five-minute prompt:

☐ Night

Midday prompt:

☐ First day at an out-of-state college for a girl who has never been away from home.

Dinner prompt:

☐ A man walks up to his boss and quits his job of twenty years. Describe the scene.

Day 65

Five-minute prompt:

☐ Soft

Midday prompt:

☐ A man has fallen in love with his best friend. The friend in question has no idea.

Dinner prompt:

☐ Strange things come out to play on moonless nights.

Day 66

Five-minute prompt:
- Strength

Midday prompt:
- A cat's guide on being a responsible human-owner.

Dinner prompt:
- Teleportation has become a reality. Write three funny scenes of teleportation gone wrong.

Day 67

Five-minute prompt:
- Steel

Midday prompt:
- A boy finds out his father is a pod-person.

Dinner prompt:
- A woman buys a dog from a local shelter, for company. The dog turns out to be a wolf. The wolf ends up turning into a person.

Day 68

Five-minute prompt:
- ☐ Burglar

Midday prompt:
- ☐ A little girl makes a silly wish on a four-leafed clover.

  It comes true.

Dinner prompt:
- ☐ Friends don't let friends get drunk and troll the FBI.

Day 69

Five-minute prompt:
- ☐ Battle

Midday prompt:
- ☐ A teenager hacks into a government database and sees something he definitely should not have.

Dinner prompt:
- ☐ A woman thinks over her marriage as she signs papers requesting a divorce.

Day 70
Five-minute prompt:
- ☐ Royal

Midday prompt:
- ☐ Life's not easy when your boss is a spoiled witch.

Dinner prompt:
- ☐ A vampire, an incubus, and a werewolf walk into a bar...

Day 71
Five-minute prompt:
- ☐ Rim

Midday prompt:
- ☐ A man finds a strange door in his basement. He cannot recall ever seeing that door before...

Dinner prompt:
- ☐ A family visits Disney Land for the first time. The parents are more excited than the kids, and the kids just want their parents to *stop embarrassing them already*!

Day 72
Five-minute prompt:
- Serenade

Midday prompt:
- Two dogs conspire to get their owners together.

Dinner prompt:
- No good deed goes unpunished. Especially when the good deed in question is taking in your neighbor's grumpy old cat.

Day 73
Five-minute prompt:
- Melancholy

Midday prompt:
- A scene from the life of a stressed-out boy-band manager.

Dinner prompt:
- Two sisters fall in love with the same man.

Day 74
Five-minute prompt:
- [ ] Malice

Midday prompt:
- [ ] A girl trades her smile for material wealth.

Dinner prompt:
- [ ] A couple has recently started living together. They are deeply in love with each other...but not with each other's idiosyncrasies, which the new living arrangement brings to light.

Day 75
Five-minute prompt:
- [ ] Thirst

Midday prompt:
- [ ] A hero becomes a villain.

Dinner prompt:
- [ ] Write a story centered around a sports game. A soccer meet, a football championship, a basketball practice - whatever you wish, as long as it is the focus of the story.

Day 76
Five-minute prompt:
- ☐ Tremble

Midday prompt:
- ☐ A super-awkward, truly adorable first date.

Dinner prompt:
- ☐ A woman is trying to learn how to cook. Her boyfriend is trying not to die via food poisoning.

Day 77
Five-minute prompt:
- ☐ Card

Midday prompt:
- ☐ The Hammurabi Code dates back to Ancient Mesopotamia (1754 BC), and is one of the oldest codes of conduct ever deciphered. Its laws encompassed all aspects of Mesopotamian society, and the punishments for transgressions were very harsh. If you had to create a Code of Conduct that would govern a society, what would it look like? What laws/punishments would it feature?

Dinner prompt:
- ☐ A boy visits the moon with his best friend (who is also an alien).

Day 78
Five-minute prompt:
- [ ] Fate

Midday prompt:
- [ ] A man travels across the globe to meet a woman he has only talked to online.

Dinner prompt:
- [ ] A blind date between two people who have in fact met before and hate each other's guts.

Day 79
Five-minute prompt:
- [ ] Queen

Midday prompt:
- [ ] Write a disjointed, chaotic story in which nothing makes sense.

Dinner prompt:
- [ ] A dog is afraid of thunder. So is his owner.

Day 80
Five-minute prompt:
- [ ] Chess

Midday prompt:
- [ ] Write a love song. Three couplets, as straightforward and honest as you can make it.

Dinner prompt:
- [ ] A little boy gets lost in the woods. Thankfully, a friendly bear finds him and helps him home.

Day 81
Five-minute prompt:
- [ ] Captive

Midday prompt:
- [ ] A journalist incidentally kidnaps the son of a famously corrupt CEO.

Dinner prompt:
- [ ] A new drug has been invented. It makes people happy, energetic, optimistic. Almost everyone takes the pill.

  Write about someone who does not use the drug, but is surrounded by people who do.

Day 82
Five-minute prompt:
- ☐ Survive

Midday prompt:
- ☐ A little boy finds a hedgehog, and decides to bring it to his kindergarten class.

Dinner prompt:
- ☐ A woman lives high in the mountains, far away from other people and civilization in general. One winter night, in the midst of a blizzard, a knock sounds on her door.

Day 83
Five-minute prompt:
- ☐ Torn

Midday prompt:
- ☐ A virtuoso musician is hiding a terrible secret: He cannot read a single note of music.

Dinner prompt:
- ☐ Two elderly women sit on a bench and gossip about their neighbors.

Day 84

Five-minute prompt:
- [ ] Talon

Midday prompt:
- [ ] A thief steals something precious from the Garden of the Sun. What is it? Does he/she manage to get away?

Dinner prompt:
- [ ] Imagine that there was in fact a place where the world ends. What would it look like?

Day 85

Five-minute prompt:
- [ ] Ares

Midday prompt:
- [ ] A woman finds a genie in a bottle.

Dinner prompt:
- [ ] Changing schools is never easy. Especially if the transition is from a private school to a barely-funded public high school.
  The son of a certain disgraced politician is about to find that out first hand.

Day 86
Five-minute prompt:
- ☐ Sign

Midday prompt:
- ☐ Grocery shopping in a store with annoyingly helpful employees.

Dinner prompt:
- ☐ An old man throws a coin in a wishing fountain. What does he wish for?

Day 87
Five-minute prompt:
- ☐ Twin

Midday prompt:
- ☐ The end of the world has come...and it is unlike anything anyone could have ever imagined.
  Write a unique scenario for the end of the world. Bonus points if it is funny.

Dinner prompt:
- ☐ Find a picture you have taken that means something to you. Write a story around it.

Day 88

Five-minute prompt:

☐ Mirror

Midday prompt:

☐ Draw something random. Once you do, flip to **Day 90** and find the rest of the prompt at the top of the page.

Dinner prompt:

☐ A young, beautiful woman suddenly grows a long, green beard.

Day 89

Five-minute prompt:

☐ Dog

Midday prompt:

☐ Write a story about a young girl whose family has recently emigrated from their native country to the United States. The girl does not speak English, and none of her classmates speak her language.

Dinner prompt:

☐ A Viking befriends a young hermit. Write of an adventure the two have together.

Midday prompt, Day 88: Whatever you have drawn is the main character in your story, and humanity's only hope against an invasion of evil faeries!

Day 90
Five-minute prompt:
- [ ] Eyes

Midday prompt:
- [ ] Introduce technology into a fairy or folk tale. Example: Red Riding Hood chatting with granny on a Smartphone, the Three Little Piglets rocking it out on DDR...

Dinner prompt:
- [ ] Two friends complain to each other about their respective significant others. By the end of their conversation, they realize they are talking about the same person.

Day 91
Five-minute prompt:
- [ ] Glaze

Midday prompt:
- [ ] An army of Teddy Bears protects a young child from monsters.

Dinner prompt:
- [ ] Describe a lazy afternoon. Focus on the mood of the story: Choose words that instill tranquility and comfort in the reader.

Day 92
Five-minute prompt:
- [ ] Barn

Midday prompt:
- [ ] A woman returns to the city in which she grew up after many years away.

Dinner prompt:
- [ ] A thin dirt road winds through a large forest. Local lore is filled with stories about people going missing after following the road in the forest's depths, and the trail itself has come to be referenced to as "the Ghost Path."

  A young man walks down the Ghost Path on a dare. An hour or so after entering the forest, he loses both the road and his way.

Day 93
Five-minute prompt:
- ☐ Cross

Midday prompt:
- ☐ A pumpkin turns into a handsome young man on Halloween Eve.

Dinner prompt:
- ☐ A man who cannot stand sweets falls in love with a baker. He goes by his crush's bakery every morning, and is inevitably forced to buy - and then consume - something sweet to gain their attention.

Day 94
Five-minute prompt:
- ☐ Curdle

Midday prompt:
- ☐ A man catches his sixteen-year-old daughter smoking. He himself is a smoker. What does he do?

Dinner prompt:
- ☐ Write a story that takes place in a society in which the color of one's eyes determines one's social class.

Day 95
Five-minute prompt:
- [ ] Faith

Midday prompt:
- [ ] A girl's pet snake is uncharacteristically loving, and extremely protective of her owner.

Dinner prompt:
- [ ] We all have a "little voice" inside our heads. Yours has escaped the confines of your mind and gained a body.

Day 96
Five-minute prompt:
- [ ] Freak

Midday prompt:
- [ ] Describe a universe that is the exact inverse of our own, in whatever capacity you choose.

Dinner prompt:
- [ ] Grab a book. Open it randomly and write down the third word in the first full sentence on the page (excluding conjunctures and the like). Do this three times.

    Write a story featuring the three words in a single sentence.

Day 97
Five-minute prompt:
- [ ] Famine

Midday prompt:
- [ ] Write a single story from three different perspectives.

Dinner prompt:
- [ ] A girl talks to her shadow. Her shadow talks back.

Day 98
Five-minute prompt:
- [ ] Mercy

Midday prompt:
- [ ] A mouse helps a cat find her way back home.

Dinner prompt:
- [ ] Write a story whose focus is not on the main action, but on surrounding happenings. For example: A robbery is occurring at a grocery store, but the story centers on a woman crossing a nearby street and touches only peripherally on the crime happening a block down.

Day 99
Five-minute prompt:
- [ ] Crocodile

Midday prompt:
- [ ] A little boy takes care of his mother while she has the flu.

Dinner prompt:
- [ ] Write a story about a character of a cultural background with which you are not familiar.

Day 100
Five-minute prompt:
- [ ] Tear

Midday prompt:
- [ ] Write a story in which both a character's outward dialogue as well as inner monologue is recorded. For example, what does a girl on a date with a not-so-suave boy think while talking with said boy?

Dinner prompt:
- [ ] A rock star falls hard for a woman he meets at a charity function. It turns out that the woman is a visiting diplomat from a foreign nation.

Day 101
Five-minute prompt:
- [ ] Drop

Midday prompt:
- [ ] Write a story composed of ten "snapshots" from a person's life.

Dinner prompt:
- [ ] In a universe where people have soulmates, a man finds his in a most inopportune moment. Namely, at a party at his superior's house, in the form of his boss' wife.

Day 102
Five-minute prompt:
- [ ] Mortal

Midday prompt:
- [ ] A girl drops through time and space, and ends up in a strange world where cat-like, humanoid creatures are the ruling race.

Dinner prompt:
- [ ] Write a story that features characters, but uses no personal pronouns.

Day 103
Five-minute prompt:
- [ ] Cerberus

Midday prompt:
- [ ] A naive man is scammed into buying a worthless property situated in the middle of a gloomy swamp. Having spent most of his life savings, he has no choice but to move there.

Dinner prompt:
- [ ] What is the silliest, most useless thing you have ever purchased? Write a story that features the item in a life-saving role.

Day 104
Five-minute prompt:
- [ ] Struck

Midday prompt:
- [ ] A man is star-struck. Literally. And an alien princess is really, really sorry.

Dinner prompt:
- [ ] You become a character in your favorite book.

Day 105
Five-minute prompt:
- [ ] Trust

Midday prompt:
- [ ] Two idiots accidentally save the world.

Dinner prompt:
- [ ] A little boy befriends the monster beneath his bed.

Day 106
Five-minute prompt:
- [ ] Dirge

Midday prompt:
- [ ] An actor has finally gotten his big break: He is to play King Arthur in a big Hollywood production.

    Only problem is, he may have bent the truth a bit when it came to the list of skills on his resume. Particularly the one to do with his mastery of horse-riding.

Dinner prompt:
- [ ] A stressed-out college senior mistakenly turns in a fanfic he/she wrote in the stead of his/her term paper.

Day 107

Five-minute prompt:

- [ ] Careen

Midday prompt:

- [ ] A boy eavesdrops on a conversation between his parents, and learns something surprising.

Dinner prompt:

- [ ] A Prince decides that he wants to be a villain rather than a hero.

  Write the story as a play.

Day 108

Five-minute prompt:

- [ ] Forgotten

Midday prompt:

- [ ] Write a story that begins with a noise. Example: BAM! BANG! THUMP!

Dinner prompt:

- [ ] Write a clichéd love story with an unexpected ending.

Day 109
Five-minute prompt:
- [ ] Triangle

Midday prompt:
- [ ] An old, grandmotherly woman is waiting in line to buy tickets for a heavy-metal concert.

Dinner prompt:
- [ ] What is the most embarrassing thing that has ever happened to you? Write a story around it.

Day 110
Five-minute prompt:
- [ ] Tar

Midday prompt:
- [ ] A detective tries to untangle a strange case: A woman has been kidnapped the night before her wedding. The groom does not seem to be too worried; neither do the woman's parents.

Dinner prompt:
- [ ] A man is playing with his dog in the park. He throws a Frisbee for the dog to chase, but when the dog comes back, it is not the Frisbee that it holds clenched between its teeth.

Day 111
Five-minute prompt:
- [ ] Fastidious

Midday prompt:
- [ ] Imagine that an important historical event never happened. What would the world be like today, if that were the case?

Dinner prompt:
- [ ] A traveler meets a kindred spirit on the road. However, as their journey progresses, strange things begin to happen - and they all seem to center around the man's new companion.

Day 112
Five-minute prompt:
- [ ] Storm

Midday prompt:
- [ ] A bandit finds a lost little girl by the side of a deserted road.

Dinner prompt:
- [ ] Meet Hedgehog and Otter, the best detective duo the world has ever seen.

Day 113
Five-minute prompt:
- [ ] Dove

Midday prompt:
- [ ] A man helps his granddaughter learn how to ride a bike.

Dinner prompt:
- [ ] A man gets stranded in the middle of nowhere, Romania. He does not speak a word of Romanian, is almost out of cash, and has no idea where he is. He resolves to walk until he hits civilization. The sun has set by the time he reaches a small village...

Day 114
Five-minute prompt:
- [ ] Beach

Midday prompt:
- [ ] Loki, the Trickster God, is a bit peeved at mortals' apparent disregard of his existence. So he does what he does best: He makes trouble.

  Unfortunately for his ego, he manages to get himself caught up in his own mischief.

Dinner prompt:
- [ ] A goddess turns into a mortal woman and walks the Earth.

Day 115
Five-minute prompt:
- Sand

Midday prompt:
- Write a story based on the following line: "Love is blind, deaf, and very, very sarcastic."

Dinner prompt:
- A man meets a strange woman in a dark forest.

Day 116
Five-minute prompt:
- Fleeting

Midday prompt:
- A man forgets his cell phone in the park. He realizes his mistake almost immediately, and is able to retrieve the phone before it disappears. When he goes back home, the man notices that there is a voicemail left on his phone. The caller is not someone he recognizes, and the message is begging the man for help in finding someone named...Mittens?

Dinner prompt:
- Personify a nation of your choosing. Give it a body, personality, and a name.

Day 117

Five-minute prompt:
- [ ] Solemn

Midday prompt:
- [ ] A King makes a foolish, selfish deal with Fate. His son must bear the consequences.

Dinner prompt:
- [ ] Write a short story that rhymes.

Day 118

Five-minute prompt:
- [ ] Heat

Midday prompt:
- [ ] Write a story that has these three elements, in order: Fall, cold, love.

Dinner prompt:
- [ ] A man has the Devil's own luck. Literally.

Day 119

Five-minute prompt:
- [ ] Moot

Midday prompt:
- [ ] Write a story that contains the following words: "the scent of roses in the air."

Dinner prompt:
- [ ] A poor man meets his Luck.

Day 120

Five-minute prompt:
- [ ] Bitter

Midday prompt:
- [ ] Write a story about a tiger in a tutu.

Dinner prompt:
- [ ] A man and his daughter live in a two-story apartment building. When the family above them moves out, an extremely rude pair of college students rents the place. The two are noisy and inconsiderate, and generally make it impossible for the man to sleep or do his work. After a week of this, the man is furious but still too polite to say anything to the troublemaking duo.

  Fortunately, his daughter does not have the same problem.

Day 121

Five-minute prompt:

☐ Bumble

Midday prompt:

☐ A little girl dresses up the family's pet cat and has a grand adventure in her grandmother's flower garden.

Dinner prompt:

☐ A girl moves to a new school. The school in question has a terrible bullying problem, especially among girls. Newcomers in particular are eaten alive.
This newcomer, however, is not someone bullies should mess with. As they are about to find out.

Day 122

Five-minute prompt:

☐ August

Midday prompt:

☐ A boy shares his sandwich with a stray dog. The dog follows him home.

Dinner prompt:

☐ A witch loses her flying broomstick. A local grandmother tries to sweep cobwebs off her ceiling, and gets quite the surprise.

Day 123
Five-minute prompt:
☐ Crumble
Midday prompt:
☐ A picnic at midnight.
Dinner prompt:
☐ Write a story based on the following anecdote:

A man was on his way back home. It was getting late, so he decided to take a shortcut through a nearby graveyard. As he walked, he could not help glancing around, a bit spooked by his surroundings.

After a short while, he caught up with a woman walking along the same path. He relaxed somewhat, happy not to be alone. The woman noticed and gave him a knowing smile.

"Don't be embarrassed," she said, "I used to be scared of graveyards too, when I was alive."

Day 124

Five-minute prompt:
☐ Paints

Midday prompt:
☐ A razor-sharp smile.

Dinner prompt:
☐ A boy gets sent to the principal's office for fighting. While waiting to be seen, he meets a girl that is there for a similar reason.

Day 125

Five-minute prompt:
☐ Smile

Midday prompt:
☐ Write a story from the perspective of a criminal.

Dinner prompt:
☐ A couple decides to have the husband be the stay-at-home parent, while the wife continues to work.

The husband quickly comes to regret this decision.

Day 126
Five-minute prompt:
- Satin

Midday prompt:
- A door-to-door salesman becomes a witness to a crime.

Dinner prompt:
- A small boy chases after a frog, loses his shoe, and ends the day by eating some dirt.

Day 127
Five-minute prompt:
- Balloon

Midday prompt:
- An accident robs a woman of her beauty. How does she face the world, after?

Dinner prompt:
- Describe an ordinary, everyday miracle.

Day 128

Five-minute prompt:
☐ Mars

Midday prompt:
☐ Write a haiku!

Traditional haiku: A poem composed of 17 syllables, divided in three lines of 5-7-5

Traditional haiku themes: Buddhism, nature, the seasons, love

Example, by a famous haiku poet:
From time to time
The clouds give rest
To the moon-beholders.
-Matsuo Bashō

Dinner prompt:
☐ The wives of two brothers cannot stand each other. Write a funny story around a family event, featuring the women's interaction.

Day 129

Five-minute prompt:
- ☐ Danger

Midday prompt:
- ☐ Superstitions are a common thread in many cultures. Describe a world in which superstitions are true, and then place a character whose luck works backwards in that world.

    For example: A black cat crossing one's path leads to bad luck in this universe; however, when that happens to your character, he/she wins the lottery.

    Here are some common superstitions:

    - **Breaking a mirror:** Seven years of bad luck (usually when it comes to love)
    - **Walking beneath a ladder:** Bad luck
    - **Saying goodbye on a bridge**: You will never see the person you said goodbye to again
    - **Opening an umbrella inside:** Brings bad luck
    - **Right hand itching:** You will be giving money soon
    - **Left hand itching:** You will be receiving money soon.

Dinner prompt:

☐ It's the year 2304. Intergalactic flight has become a possibility, with new discoveries and advances made all the time.

A young scientist signs up for a routine exploratory mission. His/her team is to visit a planet near Earth that has been found to sustain plant life. The scientist in question is very unassuming and shy - easily overlooked by the rest of the crew and senior members of the science department.

Which is probably why he/she gets left behind on the strange planet.

With its very strange inhabitants.

Who turn out not to be limited to plants.

Day 130
Five-minute prompt:
- [ ] Dark

Midday prompt:
- [ ] They say that people who grew up near the sea or ocean cannot happily live inland. Tell the story of a woman who returns to her hometown by the sea after years spent away.

Dinner prompt:
- [ ] While on vacation with her parents, a teenage girl finds a strange, gem-colored stone in the sea. She takes it home with her.

Day 131
Five-minute prompt:
- [ ] Dune

Midday prompt:
- [ ] Come up with a short monologue that can be performed by a stand-up comedian.

Dinner prompt:
- [ ] The world's best secret service agent is a fraud. Not that he/she knows it.
  Write about a secret agent who is terrible at his/her job, but has such an amazing luck that his/her missions are always unmitigated successes.

Day 132
Five-minute prompt:
- [ ] Son

Midday prompt:
- [ ] Write a story in fifty words.

Dinner prompt:
- [ ] A bunny tries to teach a cat how to hop.

Day 133
Five-minute prompt:
- [ ] Sister

Midday prompt:
- [ ] A little girl wants a puppy. After months of begging, her parents finally cave in; they take her to the local dog shelter and let her pick one of the many puppies romping around.
  The little girl falls in love with a big, scary Doberman instead.

Dinner prompt:
- [ ] Write about a personal triumph. Why was it important to you? What made it special?

Day 134

Five-minute prompt:
- [ ] Shun

Midday prompt:
- [ ] A woman in middle age is thrown back in time, into her teenage body.

Dinner prompt:
- [ ] Create a character. Give them a name, personality, physical description, and a backstory. You can structure your description so:

  Name:
  Physical appearance
    Hair color:
    Skin color:
    Eye color:
    Height:
    Weight/body shape:
    Tattoos/other:
  Personality
    Strengths:
    Weaknesses:
    Things they hate:
    Things they love:
    Governing principles/morals:
    Goals/motivation:
  Background
    Home country and city:
    Family circumstances:

Day 135
Five-minute prompt:
- [ ] Covet

Midday prompt:
- [ ] Write a story that has a sudden twist at the end. Something unexpected, yet logical within the confines of the story.

Dinner prompt:
- [ ] A preschool teacher on too-few cups of coffee tries to bring a classroom of adorable, mischievous toddlers to order.

Day 136
Five-minute prompt:
- [ ] Greed

Midday prompt:
- [ ] A musician tries to leave his management company, only to discover that the company has cheated him out of most of his earnings.

Dinner prompt:
- [ ] A duck thinks it is actually an airplane.

Day 137

Five-minute prompt:

☐ Blue

Midday prompt:

☐ In Japan, it is believed that if one folds a thousand paper cranes, their most desired wish will be granted.

A girl folds a crane every day, for a thousand days. She makes her wish as she folds the wings of the thousandth crane.

Dinner prompt:

☐ A woman receives a late-night visitor in a small, provincial town.

Write the story from two perspectives: First, from that of the woman's gossipy neighbor who sees the strange visitor knock at the woman's door. Then, from the woman's own perspective.

Day 138
Five-minute prompt:
- ☐ Bee

Midday prompt:
- ☐ An actor is chosen as the lead in a movie depicting the life of a brilliant - and quite a bit insane - nineteenth century businessman. The actor has trouble getting into character, so his agent suggests he familiarizes himself with the businessman's history. To do so, the actor travels to his character's native city and spends the weekend at the late-businessman's home, which has been turned into a museum.

    When the actor returns to the set the following Monday, he performs marvelously. He does not, however, appear to be fully himself - or *only* himself...

Dinner prompt:
- ☐ Aliens have lived on Earth for thousands of years. Some hide themselves from humans; others walk among them in disguise. A man and a woman are trapped inside a burning building. One of them is of an alien race; in order to save both of their lives, he/she needs to betray his/her secret.

Day 139

Five-minute prompt:

- [ ] Flirt

Midday prompt:

- [ ] A little girl gets lost in a field of sunflowers. A kind scarecrow shows her the way home.

Dinner prompt:

- [ ] A bratty teen is convicted of a minor crime. As the teen in question is a repeated and unapologetic offender, the judge sentences him/her to a week in actual prison as a lesson.

Day 140

Five-minute prompt:

- [ ] Sauna

Midday prompt:

- [ ] A shy boy makes a friend on his first day in kindergarten.

Dinner prompt:

- [ ] While looking through her photo album, a woman notices an unfamiliar man in the background of one of her wedding-day photos. She looks carefully through the rest of her photos and, with growing horror, realizes that the man is in every. Single. One.

Day 141
Five-minute prompt:
- [ ] Vain

Midday prompt:
- [ ] A young married couple purchases their first home. It is an astonishingly beautiful property located in a secluded nook toward the end of a small mountain town. The couple cannot believe their luck in finding the property - and receiving such a wonderful deal on it, to boot! The morning following their first day in their new home, the couple discovers the reason for the house's low price: It is strangely, unfortunately popular with the local wildlife.

Dinner prompt:
- [ ] Look around yourself. Describe the room you are in, in as great detail as possible.

Day 142

Five-minute prompt:
☐ Frost

Midday prompt:
☐ A man lives off scamming women for their money and possessions. He is an expert at emotional manipulation, and has not had so much as a single criminal charge raised against him.

His latest victim, however, proves tougher to crack than the rest. Possibly because she is a detective who has been tailing him for the past several months.

Not that her scamming beau is aware of the fact.

Dinner prompt:
☐ Write about a single day from the perspective of a dog.

Day 143
Five-minute prompt:
- ☐ Simper

Midday prompt:
- ☐ A family inadvertently adopts a squirrel.

Dinner prompt:
- ☐ In a society where men are traditionally seen as the weaker gender, a young man is getting ready for his wedding day.

Day 144
Five-minute prompt:
- ☐ Bell

Midday prompt:
- ☐ Write about a super-powered villain whose only weakness is... being hugged.

Dinner prompt:
- ☐ Write a story about your childhood home. The story can be based on a real memory, or completely fictional. Try to include as many details about the house and its surroundings as possible.

Day 145

Five-minute prompt:
- [ ] Wine

Midday prompt:
- [ ] Fill the following prompt in a genre you have never previously written in:

    While visiting her grandmother, a girl stumbles into a room she does not remember ever seeing before. The room itself seems empty, with the exception of a large, frameless mirror hung on the back wall.

Dinner prompt:
- [ ] Open your fridge. Note down the first five things you see in there.

    Write a story that features all five.

Day 146
Five-minute prompt:
- ☐ Fear

Midday prompt:
- ☐ A writer's house keeps getting invaded by a curious kitten.

The writer is allergic to cats.

Dinner prompt:
- ☐ A lion escapes from the zoo and ends up in the backyard of a local kindergarten. A little girl befriends him.

Day 147
Five-minute prompt:
- ☐ Leader

Midday prompt:
- ☐ Strange things happen when a witch sneezes.

Dinner prompt:
- ☐ Pick a character you have previously written about. Create an outfit for them and describe it in detail.

Day 148
Five-minute prompt:
- ☐ Folly

Midday prompt:
- ☐ A man is being stalked by a pink elephant that only he can see.

Dinner prompt:
- ☐ A man wakes up in a field, surrounded by curious sheep. He resolves to limit his drinking. That, or get better friends.

Day 149
Five-minute prompt:
- ☐ Pest

Midday prompt:
- ☐ A woman moves into an apartment rumored to be haunted. Turns out it is. The woman and the resident ghost end up making pretty great roommates.

Dinner prompt:
- ☐ A man sells his soul to save his life. Is it worth it, in the end?

Day 150
Five-minute prompt:
- Deluge

Midday prompt:
- Two women who do not know each other strike up a conversation on the train. They share stories about their kids, give each other advice, and generally bemoan the hardships of motherhood.

  It is not until the end of the trip that it becomes apparent one of the women had been talking about her pet cats the entire time.

Dinner prompt:
- A little girl gets into her mother's expensive make-up.

Day 151
Five-minute prompt:
- Mime

Midday prompt:
- It is 'bring your daughter to work' day. A stressed-out lawyer takes his daughter to his office. She takes her stuffed giraffe along. Everybody has a much better day as a result.

Dinner prompt:
- Write a story inspired by the following sentence: "Drowning on earth."

Day 152

Five-minute prompt:

☐ Monotone

Midday prompt:

☐ While battling a fire, a firefighter becomes trapped in a burning room. A young boy finds him just before the ceiling collapses and leads him to safety.

After being released from the hospital, the firefighter seeks out the family who owned the burned house in order to thank the boy. The family, an elderly couple, receives him warmly - and with some confusion.

They do not have a son.

Dinner prompt:

☐ A girl gets "discovered" - but not for a talent she would have ever expected.

Day 153
Five-minute prompt:
- ☐ Bud

Midday prompt:
- ☐ A woman who has not worked a day in her life finds herself joining the blue-collar workforce when her husband suddenly dies and leaves her facing bankruptcy.

Dinner prompt:
- ☐ Write a story that takes place in the waiting are of a train station.

Day 154
Five-minute prompt:
- ☐ Tingle

Midday prompt:
- ☐ Create a summary for a book you want to write.

Dinner prompt:
- ☐ An anniversary dinner turns into a total disaster. Ex-girlfriends, bad meat, faulty appliances, and nosy neighbors all make an appearance.

Day 155
Five-minute prompt:
☐ Red
Midday prompt:
☐ Two strangers escape a sudden downpour in the same tiny cafe. The coffee is bad, the service is worse; the two still fall in love.
Dinner prompt:
☐ A grown man cries over something silly.

Day 156
Five-minute prompt:
☐ Tread
Midday prompt:
☐ A computer geek falls in love with a technology-challenged tech-support client.
Dinner prompt:
☐ Mothers have the (at times, annoying) habit of being right. Write a story in which a mother has the cause to say "I told you so" to her willful child.

Day 157

Five-minute prompt:
☐ Path

Midday prompt:
☐ A child receives a phone call from his/her deployed parent. Write their conversation, dialogue-only.

Dinner prompt:
☐ A teenage girl is feeling a bit down in the wake of moving to a new school. She goes to the local mall to cheer herself up

The following happens, in no specific order:
- The bus she is on breaks down.
- She loses her phone.
- A seagull steals her sandwich.
- She befriends a ninja.

It is the best day she's had in a long time.

Day 158
Five-minute prompt:
- [ ] Forest

Midday prompt:
- [ ] A woman quits her job and starts her own knitting business online.

Dinner prompt:
- [ ] An alien ship accidentally abducts a man as it passes over his house.

Day 159
Five-minute prompt:
- [ ] Fair

Midday prompt:
- [ ] A fair princess loses her beauty to a curse. It's the best thing that has ever happened to her.

Dinner prompt:
- [ ] Write a haunted house story from the perspective of the ghosts.

Day 160
Five-minute prompt:
- [ ] Tale

Midday prompt:
- [ ] Do you speak another language? If you do, write a story in which at least part of the conversation is in that language.

  If you do not, choose a language you have studied - or always wanted to study - and try to include as many coherent sentences in it as you can in your story.

Dinner prompt:
- [ ] A brilliant woman who works in a meaningless, low-paid job finally gets her lucky break.

Day 161
Five-minute prompt:
- [ ] Lie

Midday prompt:
- [ ] A little kid and a bear cub share a jar of honey. Their respective mothers are quite perplexed on what to do.

Dinner prompt:
- [ ] After a night of drinking, a brave warrior faces his biggest challenge yet: His furious wife.

Day 162

Five-minute prompt:
☐ Sworn

Midday prompt:
☐ The night before their wedding, a young couple receives much-unwanted marriage advice.

Write the story in three parts: The first should focus on the young bride and her mother. The second should feature the young man and his father. The third describes the wedding.

Dinner prompt:
☐ A CEO takes up knitting for relaxation. It works, for the most part. Plus, there's the added bonus of instilling fear in his subordinates as they watch him crochet furiously during his lunch breaks.

Day 163

Five-minute prompt:
☐ Brother

Midday prompt:
☐ A man and a woman are in a relationship. Both want to end it, but believe the other is still in love and will be hurt. Write a humorous story about their attempts to let each other down easy.

Dinner prompt:
☐ A family is sick of rude telemarketers. So they make a game out of confusing and bewildering unwanted callers.

Describe four such calls, one for each family member.

Day 164
Five-minute prompt:
☐ Misery

Midday prompt:
☐ A string of bank robberies leaves the local police baffled. No matter how fast they are or how many security cameras the given bank has, the thieves are never seen or caught. An inside job begins to seem more and more likely.

Dinner prompt:
☐ A superhero and a super villain are best friends in their daily lives. Neither is aware of the other's secret identity.

Day 165
Five-minute prompt:
- [ ] Rise

Midday prompt:
- [ ] An overworked secretary finally snaps and gives her boss a piece of her mind.

Dinner prompt:
- [ ] A race of humans believed to have gone extinct some time before the birth of the first homo-sapien is discovered still very much alive and well at a secluded and previously unknown island. A team composed of scientists and military personnel is sent in to make contact.

Day 166
Five-minute prompt:
☐ Rove
Midday prompt:
☐ A cat blackmails its owners for food and cat stuff and general household dominance.
Dinner prompt:
☐ A man is let go from his job when his company downsizes. He is unable to find another job in his profession, so he has to temporarily settle for a menial position. Too embarrassed to tell his family, the man pretends he still works at his old office when he is in fact flipping burgers at a local fast-food place.

Day 167

Five-minute prompt:

☐ Raven

Midday prompt:

☐ *Gulliver's Travels* by Jonathan Swift is, among other things, a tremendously creative and imaginative work. If you were to write a similar book of travel and discovery, where would you send your characters? What would you have them discover?

Write a scene, or otherwise compose a list of fictional places, peoples, and fauna you would include in such a story.

Dinner prompt:

☐ Little Red Riding Hood goes into the forest on her way to visit her grandmother. Only she does not meet the Big Bad Wolf, but the Sassy Red Fox. The two have some great adventures together.

Day 168
Five-minute prompt:
- Headless

Midday prompt:
- A beautiful golden urn is unearthed at the outskirts of a small Eastern European town. It is a gorgeous, valuable artifact left from an ancient civilization. It is also not empty.

Dinner prompt:
- An amateur photographer accidentally takes a photo of a corrupt cop making a deal with a local gangster.

Day 169
Five-minute prompt:
- Shore

Midday prompt:
- A woman's "third eye" opens. Literally, and in the middle of her forehead.

Dinner prompt:
- Imagine dinosaurs were actually dragons, and that folk lore related to the fire-breathing beasts is true. Write a story of an ancient civilization's interaction with the giant lizards.

Day 170
Five-minute prompt:
- [ ] Crop

Midday prompt:
- [ ] A man falls asleep beneath a cherry tree heavy with fruit. Night has already fallen when he wakes up. He makes to get up - and hears strange, hissing voices above him.
The man looks up, and sees...

Dinner prompt:
- [ ] A woman leaves her husband and children, leaving behind only a letter to explain her decision.
Write that letter.

Day 171
Five-minute prompt:
- [ ] Grave

Midday prompt:
- [ ] A small, dense forest is rumored to be the meeting place of strange, dark things. One full-moon night, two teenage boys decide to find out if the rumors are true.

Dinner prompt:
- [ ] A day at the Aquarium turns hilariously chaotic when a giant octopus escapes its tank.

Day 172
Five-minute prompt:
- [ ] Vicious

Midday prompt:
- [ ] A day in the life of a misanthropic telepath.

Dinner prompt:
- [ ] Before the existence of post offices and telephone lines, letters and news of importance were entrusted to Messengers. Write a story about a Messenger who bears the news of an enemy invasion and his desperate run to his nation's capital and King.

Day 173
Five-minute prompt:
- [ ] Vivid

Midday prompt:
- [ ] A girl hears colors in sound - be it music, people's voices, or the rustling of leaves. Write a story about how she perceives the world and its inhabitants.

Dinner prompt:
- [ ] A vampire bemoans the shameful way in which his race is being depicted in contemporary pop-culture.

Day 174
Five-minute prompt:
- ☐ Cost

Midday prompt:
- ☐ A woman overly-concerned with other people's opinions is dreadfully embarrassed of her carefree sister. Said sister could not care less.

Dinner prompt:
- ☐ Write a story of star-crossed lovers, with an unexpected and unorthodox twist at the end.

Day 175
Five-minute prompt:
- ☐ Lily

Midday prompt:
- ☐ A man tries to buy his wife an anniversary present that she will, for once, actually like. "Tries" being the keyword.

Dinner prompt:
- ☐ A man attempts to be "cool" in front of his son's friends. The results are embarrassingly humorous.

Day 176

Five-minute prompt:
- [ ] Harvest

Midday prompt:
- [ ] A college grad is looking for a job and has, in growing desperation, applied to everything from burger joints to corporate offices. Describe several interviews he/she goes to. Try to make them as comically awful as possible.

Dinner prompt:
- [ ] A foreign exchange student is trying to get used to the local culture. His/her host family is ridiculously enthusiastic about helping him/her do so. They are also very ignorant of the student's own culture, and bombard him/her with well-meant but often strange questions.

Day 177

Five-minute prompt:

☐ Rambunctious

Midday prompt:

☐ A college professor is reading through an essay exam most of his students failed. Describe several amusingly terrible responses, and the professor's reaction to them.

Dinner prompt:

☐ A woman is robbed of her dream of becoming an actress when she is attacked and disfigured by what she believes to have been a rabid dog.

The following full moon, she realizes something else altogether has happened to her.

Day 178
Five-minute prompt:
☐ Sly

Midday prompt:
☐ A busy, overworked father imagines what his life would have been like, had he not gotten married.

Dinner prompt:
☐ A monk falls in love with a woman he chances upon while collecting apples in the monastery's orchard. He begins to seriously reconsider his vows.

There is, however, more to that woman than first meets the eye.

Day 179
Five-minute prompt:
☐ Pretty

Midday prompt:
☐ Two friends make everything into a competition. Including baking cookies for a tea party that they have both been invited to.

Dinner prompt:
☐ Write the hypothetical schedule of a full-time housewife with two children and one forgetful husband.

Day 180

Five-minute prompt:

☐ Fruitless

Midday prompt:

☐ A sailor goes overboard during a terrible storm. He loses consciousness, only to wake up surrounded by strange people on an unknown island. The man does not understand the language the people speak, and the people have never heard of the man's native land.

Dinner prompt:

☐ A child disappears while playing with a friend in its own backyard. The friend seems terrified and refuses to speak. The local police cannot find a trace of the child, or any indication that the child had at any point left his/her family's property.

Day 181

Five-minute prompt:
- Silver

Midday prompt:
- A woman buys a pet pig.
  Her long-suffering roommate seriously considers selling it to the local butcher.

Dinner prompt:
- Write a story from the perspective of an individual who is disturbingly obsessed with someone.

Day 182

Five-minute prompt:
- Horns

Midday prompt:
- A woman goes to a tarot-cards reader in hopes of receiving advice for her love life. The woman she usually goes to is absent; in her place is a stunningly handsome man.
  The woman forgets all about her romance woes.

Dinner prompt:
- A woman accidentally pepper-sprays her boss.

Day 183

Five-minute prompt:
- ☐ Halo

Midday prompt:
- ☐ Drunk chickens.

Dinner prompt:
- ☐ The following is a real question found on an application for entrance to a Master's degree program in a prestigious U.S. University. Answer it.

  Describe an event or experience in which you exercised a significant decision-making, management, or leadership role. (750 word limit)

Day 184

Five-minute prompt:

- [ ] Sturdy

Midday prompt:

- [ ] In a fictional country still ruled by a monarch, a political faction within the government has the King secretly assassinated. They believe the King's son will be easy to control, thus allowing them more power within the country.

    When the Queen rather than the Prince succeeds the throne, the traitors find they may have bitten more than they can chew.

Dinner prompt:

- [ ] A divorced couple juggles their kids, bills, and their own messy feelings.

Day 185
Five-minute prompt:
☐ Stain
Midday prompt:
☐ A man discovers a photograph of a beautiful girl tucked in one of his old textbooks. A name is scrawled on the back of the aged photo. Unable to recall neither the girl nor why he has her picture, the man decides to look her up.
Dinner prompt:
☐ They say dogs look like their owners. Write a story in which a good-natured Great Dane watches on in confusion as a tiny Pincher barks enthusiastically at him. In the background, the same scene repeats with the dogs' owners.

Day 186
Five-minute prompt:
- ☐ Lure

Midday prompt:
- ☐ A boy from a poor family makes it into one of the most exclusive schools in his country. He is there on a scholarship, and everyone else is very aware of the fact.

Dinner prompt:
- ☐ A man witnesses a father viciously castigating his son. The boy flinches constantly, hinting at further abuse.

The man steps in.

Day 187
Five-minute prompt:
- ☐ Pepper

Midday prompt:
- ☐ A detective is trying to interview an astonishingly conceited, dense woman in connection to a crime. The woman is convinced the detective is flirting with her.

Dinner prompt:
- ☐ The personal assistant of an important politician notices something strange about some of his boss' financial supporters.

Day 188
Five-minute prompt:
- [ ] Spice

Midday prompt:
- [ ] A supermodel falls in love with her shy, geeky agent.

Dinner prompt:
- [ ] A camping trip turns surreal when a terrible storm forces a family to take shelter in a cave... and bunk with its furry inhabitants.

Day 189
Five-minute prompt:
- [ ] Sorrow

Midday prompt:
- [ ] A wizard accidentally turns his wife into a crow.

  He kind of wishes she had taken a different form. Something without a beak would have been much preferred.

Dinner prompt:
- [ ] A woman meets her husband's lover.

Day 190
Five-minute prompt:
- ☐ Creep

Midday prompt:
- ☐ A fancy tea party is ruined by a band of vindictive clowns.

Dinner prompt:
- ☐ A character gains the ability to turn invisible. What is the first thing they do with it?

Day 191
Five-minute prompt:
- ☐ Spoil

Midday prompt:
- ☐ A boy happy with life on his family's farm is sent to a boarding school in a far-away city.

Dinner prompt:
- ☐ Two powerful families arrange for their children to wed. The future groom and bride meet a week before their wedding. It is hate at first sight.

Day 192
Five-minute prompt:
- [ ] Corporate

Midday prompt:
- [ ] Being a doctor is difficult. Being the nurse assisting a grouchy doctor is even more-so.

Dinner prompt:
- [ ] Write a story about a person running a marathon in a way that properly conveys the experience of running long-distance. Make the text exhausting - either to read (long sentences, etc.) or in terms of adjectives and description.

Day 193
Five-minute prompt:
- [ ] Machine

Midday prompt:
- [ ] An airplane pilot sees something extraordinary in the sky.

Dinner prompt:
- [ ] While pulling off a high-stakes heist at a gangster's home, a thief steals something that was not on the agenda. "Someone," actually.

Day 194

Five-minute prompt:
- Train

Midday prompt:
- There is only one thing to do when your spendthrift son ends up moving back home for the fifth time: Find him a wife. The candidates for the position - all friends or ex-girlfriends of the man - are less than impressed.

Dinner prompt:
- A woman finds out the company she has worked in for over thirty years plans to let her go.

Day 195
Five-minute prompt:
☐ Lost
Midday prompt:
☐ The boogeyman discusses the hardships of his job in a late-night show interview.
Dinner prompt:
☐ A hiker encounters a terrible winter storm while high up on a mountain. Disorientated and unable to make contact with anyone on the ground, he takes cover in a shallow cave to wait the storm out.

Someone else has done the same thing, and the hiker is surprised to find he is not alone on the mountain.

Day 196

Five-minute prompt:

☐ Island

Midday prompt:

☐ A down-on-his-luck man is sitting on a bus stop, waiting for a bus that is to take him to yet another job interview. An older man sits beside him. After several minutes, the older man begins to talk: He questions the young man about his troubles and gives him advice. The advice in question seems strange to the younger man, but he decides to follow it. His life changes around almost immediately.

Dinner prompt:

☐ A grocery store clerk helps a lost little boy find his mother.

Day 197
Five-minute prompt:
☐ Teal
Midday prompt:
☐ Make up a riddle!
Dinner prompt:
☐ A girl kisses a boy on a dare.

Day 198
Five-minute prompt:
☐ Mark
Midday prompt:
☐ A group of college friends meet again after ten years apart. Life has changed a lot for all of them, but it has not changed them or their friendship.
Dinner prompt:
☐ A sweet woman turns grouchy when sick. Her boyfriend is not prepared for the transformation.

Day 199

Five-minute prompt:
☐ Bridge

Midday prompt:
☐ A week lost at sea has a sailor losing his mind.

Dinner prompt:
☐ The Chinese Almanac is means of telling auspicious and inauspicious days, hours, and directions of travel. It was widely used in both feudal Japan and China, and is still popular with esoteric healers.

Tell a story in which the Hour of the Ox (the time between 1 am and 3 am) is featured. If you would like the story to be more accurate, check the site below for the day's Almanac and whether the Hour of the Ox happens to be auspicious or not.

Link:
http://www.dragon-gate.com/tool/almanac/

Day 200
Five-minute prompt:
- [ ] Gap

Midday prompt:
- [ ] A woman decides to give her unborn child up for adoption.

Dinner prompt:
- [ ] Instead of performing the song that had been assigned to him, a boy sings something he had created for the girl he secretly likes during a school assembly.

Day 201
Five-minute prompt:
- [ ] Song

Midday prompt:
- [ ] A man finds the gate to the Underworld. The heavy doors are slightly parted. Curious, the man leans in and tries to see what lies hidden behind them...

Dinner prompt:
- [ ] Write a short story about a day in the life of a Flight Agent. Flight delays, rude customers, and lazy co-workers abound!

Day 202
Five-minute prompt:
- [ ] Heart

Midday prompt:
- [ ] In the wake of a tragedy, a man decides that it is better to not have a heart than to have it broken.

Dinner prompt:
- [ ] A toddler teaches his/her stressed-out parent that being messy is okay, sometimes. Kind of fun, too!

Day 203
Five-minute prompt:
- [ ] Belief

Midday prompt:
- [ ] Describe a place of rest and peace - such as a church, a forest, or a garden - late at night. Toe the line between calm and creepy with your description.

Dinner prompt:
- [ ] A woman leaves law-school in order to pursue her dream of becoming a pastry-chef. She is a terrible cook, but it all works out anyway.

Day 204

Five-minute prompt:
☐ Comply

Midday prompt:
☐ There is a strange little house at the end of a quiet suburban street. It's fences are tall, its sides overgrown with ivy and weeds, and the brown paint of its window-ledges has chipped and faded all over. No one ever goes in or out, and the mailman never stops by its rusted mailbox.

Yet, there is always a light on behind one of the dust-heavy second-floor windows.

Dinner prompt:
☐ Write a story inspired by this nursery rhyme:

Monday's child is fair of face;
Tuesday's child is full of grace;
Wednesday's child is full of woe;
Thursday's child has far to go;
Friday's child is loving and giving;
Saturday's child works hard for a living. But the child that is born on the Sabbath day
is fair and wise, good and gay.

Day 205

Five-minute prompt:
- [ ] Ship

Midday prompt:
- [ ] Greed tears two brothers apart when they discover a chest filled with gold buried in their late-father's back yard.

Dinner prompt:
- [ ] Have you ever had to memorize a poem for school? If so, try to recall as much of it as you can. Use the lines you remember in a story. If not, write a story featuring a poem that holds personal meaning for you.

Day 206
Five-minute prompt:
☐ Sea
Midday prompt:
☐ James Joyce's incredibly complex novel, *Ulysses*, is based upon the premises of Homer's *The Odyssey* in that it depicts the journey of a man to his home.

Write a story that is, at its heart, one of journeying "back home" - in whatever capacity you choose.
Dinner prompt:
☐ A girl bullied terribly at school stumbles upon a strange website that promises to solve all of her troubles.

Day 207

Five-minute prompt:
- [ ] Trudge

Midday prompt:
- [ ] The following is believed in cultures across Europe: If you hear your name called out late at night you should not turn around, for it might be the Devil calling you.

    One dark night, a man is alone in his home when he hears someone calling his name. He turns around.

Dinner prompt:
- [ ] A woman suffering from severe agoraphobia (fear of situations and places that may cause unpleasantness, often resulting in fear of the outside world as a whole) has not left her home in over ten years. One day, she sees an unfamiliar van parked in front of her neighbor's home. The neighbor's two children are playing outside. The driver of the van beckons them over. The children go closer to the van.

    Realizing what is happening, the woman finds herself in a nerve-wrecking situation and only minutes to overcome her terror of the world beyond her doorstep.

Day 208
Five-minute prompt:
☐ Hill
Midday prompt:
☐ Baba Yaga is a well-known character in Russian folklore. Usually described as an old, powerful sorceress living in a hut balanced upon a single chicken-leg, Baba Yaga is a mercurial being: At times cruel, at times benevolent.

Write a story about a child who stumbles upon Baba Yaga's hut.
Dinner prompt:
☐ A blackmailing ring targets a popular singer with a net-worth in the millions of dollars. The job is to be a quick profit: The singer in question is known to be an utter airhead, and the blackmailers expect her to bend at the slightest pressure.

Unfortunately for the criminals, the singer's "dumb-blonde" persona is completely staged. The woman beneath the make-up and outrageous outfits is in fact quite shrewd - as well as very, very vindictive.

Day 209
Five-minute prompt:
- [ ] City

Midday prompt:
- [ ] A woman finds a beautiful golden necklace. Rubies and diamonds weave along it - as do strange runes that feel warm to the touch.

Dinner prompt:
- [ ] An old sinner prays for absolution. At the same time, a pious young man commits a grave crime.

Day 210
Five-minute prompt:
- [ ] Daunting

Midday prompt:
- [ ] A duck waddles into a library.

Dinner prompt:
- [ ] A train accident leaves a close-minded businessman stranded in a small, developing nation.

Day 211

Five-minute prompt:
☐ Duck

Midday prompt:
☐ Two ships pass by one another on a dark, moonless night. The captain of one of the ships hails the other.
No one responds.

Dinner prompt:
☐ A young woman inherits an enormous mansion from her great-great-aunt, along with the rest of the deceased's considerable earthly possessions. The only stipulation to receiving the fortune is that the young woman make the mansion her home. The woman is more than happy to comply.
That is of course before she actually sees her creepy new home.

Day 212

Five-minute prompt:

☐ Bundle

Midday prompt:

☐ Write a story in which a wife has reason to call her husband "idiot" at least four times.

Dinner prompt:

☐ Describe a winter festival, fictitious or real. Try to capture the excitement of the event and the warmth of peoples enjoyment. Juxtapose it with the coldness of the season.

Day 213

Five-minute prompt:

☐ Last

Midday prompt:

☐ An Army veteran visits a monument built to commemorate the soldiers who have fallen in a certain war. The names carved in the stone are ones the man knows well.

Dinner prompt:

☐ While sight-seeing in a foreign city a tourist gets lost, robbed, chased by a pretty girl's angry fiancé, and even catches on fire for a little bit.

All in all, it's an unforgettable experience.

Day 214
Five-minute prompt:
☐ Corrode

Midday prompt:
☐ A girl forgets her phone at home. Her mother "accidentally" goes through her messages. Long story short, a certain secret boyfriend is invited to (interrogation) dinner.

Dinner prompt:
☐ Pick a character from a story you have previously written. Switch their gender. Write a new story featuring that character in his or her new body.

Day 215

Five-minute prompt:

☐ Loop

Midday prompt:

☐ Meeting a girl's parents for the first time is always nerve-wrecking. When said parents are a decorated Army General and a Special Ops agent, it's a downright heart stopping experience. Possibly literally.

Dinner prompt:

☐ A murder mystery leaves a small-town police force baffled. The police Chief contacts the federal government for assistance. What he gets is a tiny, messy, psychotic woman with an FBI badge and the title of the best investigator the agency's ever seen.

Day 216
Five-minute prompt:
- ☐ Cradle

Midday prompt:
- ☐ Write ten disjointed sentences.

  ...

  Done? Now include all of them in the same story.

Dinner prompt:
- ☐ A man is awoken in the middle of the night by the mad barking of his neighbor's dog. Disoriented and grumpy, the man opens his bedroom window with the full intent of screaming himself hoarse at the stupid mutt.

  His breath catches in his throat when he sees at what the dog is barking.

Day 217

Five-minute prompt:
☐ Hoard

Midday prompt:
☐ Write a story that includes the following exclamation:
"Watch out for the monkey!"

Dinner prompt:
☐ J.R.R. Tolkien will forever be remembered for the wondrous worlds and characters he created. Among Tolkien's many literary accomplishments is the creation of several languages, all with their own linguistic roots and grammar.

Create an alphabet for a fictional language. Name the language and ascribe it to a race of peoples or creatures.

Day 218

Five-minute prompt:
☐ Smoke

Midday prompt:
☐ Two mothers drink coffee in one of the women's living rooms. Their two young children are playing nearby. The mothers are discussing their children.

Several feet away, their children are discussing the mothers.

Dinner prompt:
☐ Two sisters, five and seven each, attempt to bake cookies while their mother takes a nap.

An oil-soaked carpet, a ceiling sticky with cookie-dough, and a visit from the fire department later the mother swears off naps - and possibly cookies - for the foreseeable future.

Day 219
Five-minute prompt:
- Home

Midday prompt:
- Write a break-up story. No crying, no hysterics - just a soft, quiet melancholy.

Dinner prompt:
- After losing her job, a woman goes out drinking with friends. She wakes up in someone's bed, hung-over and very much married - to what turns out to be her ex-boss.

Day 220
Five-minute prompt:
- Sweet

Midday prompt:
- People don't change; they just become more themselves with time.

  Write a story that explores the above.

Dinner prompt:
- A Healer is asked to visit a small village in which a strange sickness wrecks havoc.

Day 221
Five-minute prompt:
- Statue

Midday prompt:
- A basketball coach watches on in despair as the few students who have come to basketball try-outs attempt to outdo one another in clumsiness.

Dinner prompt:
- A woman breaks her arm, loses her job, and is almost evicted from her apartment. Then she runs into a handsome stranger at her doctor's office. Her life does a one-eighty.

Day 222
Five-minute prompt:
- Master

Midday prompt:
- A statue comes to life.

Dinner prompt:
- Describe a day filled with fireworks, good food, and laughter - all of life's best things.

Day 223
Five-minute prompt:
- [ ] Shell

Midday prompt:
- [ ] A man finds a strange box buried beneath a pile of clothing and shoes in his wife's closet. The box is locked; a note taped to its side reads: "If you open the box, I'm divorcing you."

Dinner prompt:
- [ ] Working in a funeral home can get pretty boring. Then there are those days when a corpse comes to life...

Day 224
Five-minute prompt:
- [ ] Hollow

Midday prompt:
- [ ] Growing up in a small town is not easy. There's gossip, drama, constant intrigue over the silliest of things, and if you even *think* about liking someone...

    Well, it's safe to say the whole town will know within hours, your crush included.

Dinner prompt:
- [ ] Three not-so-bright individuals discuss world happenings over beer.

Day 225

Five-minute prompt:

☐ Dry

Midday prompt:

☐ In some cultures, it is believed that an even number of flowers is only offered at funerals. A man not aware of this belief gifts his foreign girlfriend with a dozen roses.

Dinner prompt:

☐ Without her morning coffee, a woman is an almost literal zombie. One morning, said woman is running late and does not have time for her much-needed shot of caffeine. Which is why she says yes when her boyfriend of two weeks asks her to marry him.

Day 226

Five-minute prompt:

☐ Sleepless

Midday prompt:

☐ Make a list of ten books that have been influential in your life.

Dinner prompt:

☐ A bulldog is not the most reliable security system.

Day 227
Five-minute prompt:
- ☐ Chosen

Midday prompt:
- ☐ A silly wolf plays with a little girl in a park while her mother reads a trashy romance on a nearby bench.

Dinner prompt:
- ☐ Write a story featuring a germophobe in a European country where cheek-kissing is the normal means of greeting.

Day 228
Five-minute prompt:
- ☐ Stale

Midday prompt:
- ☐ An aging actress takes an embarrassing role in the hopes of recapturing her previous fame.

Dinner prompt:
- ☐ A dog saves its owner from the evil, loud, things-sucking machine (aka: the vacuum).

Day 229

Five-minute prompt:

☐ Drawn

Midday prompt:

☐ Quitting smoking is not easy. Grumpiness is not the worst possible side effect of nicotine withdrawal, but it is definitely in the running. Especially when one is at their annoying boss' house for dinner.

Dinner prompt:

☐ At a high-end store, a snobby sales representative insults person after person. He is especially vicious toward a bookish-looking woman, not realizing that she is the daughter of the store's owner.

Day 230
Five-minute prompt:
☐ Possess

Midday prompt:
☐ A garbage man discovers something strange at a residential dumpster.

Dinner prompt:
☐ A pizza boy has his weirdest house visit yet.

Day 231
Five-minute prompt:
☐ Precious

Midday prompt:
☐ A little boy builds a fort out of his grandfather's prized book collection. The grandfather is torn between tears and laughter.

Dinner prompt:
☐ A noble in the French Court under Louis XIV falls in love with one of the King's mistresses.

Day 232
Five-minute prompt:
- [ ] Simple

Midday prompt:
- [ ] A little boy finds a lizard while playing in the park and puts it in his mother's purse. The mother gets a surprise while looking for her wallet in the grocery store.

Dinner prompt:
- [ ] A girl gets to meet her biggest idol. It's unfortunate that it happens during the most embarrassing moment in her life.

Day 233
Five-minute prompt:
- [ ] Fairy

Midday prompt:
- [ ] During an office party, a section manager introduces his wife. His subordinates cannot believe their eyes; what is a beautiful, gregarious woman doing with their grumpy boss?

Dinner prompt:
- [ ] A young boy sees snow for the first time. He thinks it is cotton and jumps right in the biggest pile of snow he can find.

Day 234
Five-minute prompt:
- Sow

Midday prompt:
- A superstar gets spotted by fans while trying to do some grocery shopping. He narrowly escapes being mobbed by adoring fans and ends up hiding in a back storage room with an employee who may or may not be high.

Dinner prompt:
- A girl selling flowers on a bridge has a strange customer one late September afternoon.

Day 235
Five-minute prompt:
- Stitch

Midday prompt:
- Write a short story of an accidental meeting between two people who used to once be in love.

Dinner prompt:
- There are many wonderful teachers out there. And then there are those who go to work only to get their paycheck.
  Write a story featuring a bad teacher and a class bored out of their minds.

Day 236
Five-minute prompt:
- Human

Midday prompt:
- A girl/boy from a small, homogenous town moves to a metropolis filled with people from all over the world.

Dinner prompt:
- A witch is seeking an assistant. Pay negotiable, hours flexible. May involve activities of dubious legality.

Day 237
Five-minute prompt:
- Want

Midday prompt:
- A sleepy news-anchor completely botches a story on live TV, with hilarious results.

Dinner prompt:
- Two whiny kids meet their new babysitter: A small, sweet-looking lady. The kids take bets on how long it will take to make her cry. They are in for a big surprise.

Day 238

Five-minute prompt:
- Dear

Midday prompt:
- *Die Toteninsel*, or "Isle of the Dead," is a famous painting by artist Arnold Böcklin (1827-1901). The painting was immensely popular with its Central European public, and continues to be of symbolic importance in contemporary film and literature. A copy of a version of the paining is found below. Write a story based on or inspired by this painting.

Dinner prompt:
- An exasperated editor is haranguing a famous but lazy author for a final draft of his latest book. Which was due about a week ago.

Day 239

Five-minute prompt:

☐ Bustle

Midday prompt:

☐ Only two people come to a man's funeral. One of them is his mother. The other, when asked, says: "I am only here to make sure he's really dead."

Dinner prompt:

☐ Write a story that includes the following: Two owls hooting on a roof, one pre-finals college student trying to sleep, and a bemused police officer answering a call about a crazy person throwing shoes at birds whilst screaming in Latin.

Day 240

Five-minute prompt:

☐ Circus

Midday prompt:

☐ Two kids playing on the beach discover a strange little creature.

Dinner prompt:

☐ An author is mortified when a trashy book he/she wrote for some quick cash tops the NY Times Bestseller's List.

Day 241
Five-minute prompt:
- [ ] Enigma

Midday prompt:
- [ ] A man attempts to take care of his wife while she is sick with the flu. He mostly fails.

Dinner prompt:
- [ ] List five things that you like to do, and why.

Day 242
Five-minute prompt:
- [ ] Desert

Midday prompt:
- [ ] A heist gone wrong, a death, and honor among thieves.

Dinner prompt:
- [ ] A family is looking for a new couch. Cue slick salesmen and unimaginably ugly divans.

Day 243
Five-minute prompt:
- [ ] Pearl

Midday prompt:
- [ ] A cat napping on a sun-drenched windowsill wonders why her owners are always so grumpy. Don't they have a nice place to nap?

Dinner prompt:
- [ ] A father teaches his sixteen-year-old daughter to drive. It's pretty much a disaster.

Day 244
Five-minute prompt:
- [ ] Sunk

Midday prompt:
- [ ] A fight breaks out in a bar. Describe the scene. Try to create a sense of fast-paced violence.

Dinner prompt:
- [ ] Write a story of colors. No matter what you choose as your subject, focus on the colors in the story. Make them the most vivid part of your writing.

Day 245
Five-minute prompt:
☐ Saddle
Midday prompt:
☐ Write a story that features a stereotypical character, in whatever capacity you wish. Make him/her adhere to all the clichés about his/her "kind," until the very end of the story where he/she acts completely out of character.
Dinner prompt:
☐ The passage of time depends on one's perception.

Write about a single day from two different perspectives: That of a fruit fly and of a turtle.

Day 246
Five-minute prompt:
☐ Compromise
Midday prompt:
☐ Write a cheesy graduation speech filled with clichés.
Dinner prompt:
☐ A man grows a beard. His wife is not thrilled.

Day 247

Five-minute prompt:
- [ ] Capricious

Midday prompt:
- [ ] A runaway kitten wrecks havoc during a domestic flight.

Dinner prompt:
- [ ] A brilliant but socially-inept boy attempts to ask his crush out on a date. After some painful mumbling and fidgeting, she takes pity and kisses him.

Day 248

Five-minute prompt:
- [ ] Champion

Midday prompt:
- [ ] Write a story of a tattoo gone hilariously wrong.

Dinner prompt:
- [ ] A man buys a used car and finds something strange in the trunk.

Day 249
Five-minute prompt:
- [ ] Trunk

Midday prompt:
- [ ] Write a story in two time periods: One in the present, one in the past, featuring the same characters at different points in their lives.

Dinner prompt:
- [ ] A girl encounters a wolf on her way back from a nearby river.

Day 250
Five-minute prompt:
- [ ] Gramophone

Midday prompt:
- [ ] Describe a precious childhood memory. Write with as much detail as you can.

Dinner prompt:
- [ ] Where would you live, if you could choose? Why?

    It can be a real or a fictitious place.

Day 251
Five-minute prompt:
- ☐ Glass

Midday prompt:
- ☐ A cat and a dog are transformed into humans. Their owner is most bemused.

Dinner prompt:
- ☐ A priest is sent to minister over a small town on the outskirts of a large kingdom. When he arrives, the priest discovers that the townsfolk continue to adhere to a number of pagan beliefs and rituals. One of them in particular strikes him as strange - and quite a bit disquieting.

Day 252
Five-minute prompt:
- ☐ Courage

Midday prompt:
- ☐ On a hot, sleepless night, a woman wakes up to the smell of something burning and rustling beneath her bed.

Dinner prompt:
- ☐ Third time's the charm!
  Or so hopes Mr. Wilson, about to be married for the third time in as many years.

Day 253
Five-minute prompt:
☐ Footstep
Midday prompt:
☐ An old man reminiscences about his youth while watching his grandson at play.
Dinner prompt:
☐ A man whose father was a gambler visits a casino. Describe his reaction to the people inside, the atmosphere, and the memories of his father the casino brings back.

Day 254
Five-minute prompt:
☐ Notes
Midday prompt:
☐ Write a story about a character incapable of feeling romantic love.
Dinner prompt:
☐ A comedian goes on a blind date. The date is really, really awkward; it does not help that he cannot seem to stop himself from making terrible jokes.

Day 255
Five-minute prompt:
- [ ] Fang

Midday prompt:
- [ ] A psychologist is psychoanalyzed by one of his patients. The psychologist is not amused.

Dinner prompt:
- [ ] A man-made virus has been accidentally released, leading to the total annihilation of 95% of the world's human population. The survivors are scattered across the globe, and find themselves no longer completely human.

Day 256
Five-minute prompt:
- [ ] Barrel

Midday prompt:
- [ ] A pathological liar weaves an intricate - and quite fictional - story for a group of naive admirers at a party. His best friend watches on with a mixture of amusement and exasperation.

Dinner prompt:
- [ ] A set of identical twins completely opposite in character decide to switch places with each other for a day.

Day 257

Five-minute prompt:
- [ ] Cumbersome

Midday prompt:
- [ ] "There is good to be found in every evil." Write a story in which the above holds true.

Dinner prompt:
- [ ] A hunter spots a large red fox. After several hours of tracking and careful herding, he corners the beast.
  Only to watch it transform into a beautiful woman.

Day 258

Five-minute prompt:
- [ ] Lacquer

Midday prompt:
- [ ] "Whatever you do, you do it to yourself." In other words: Write a karma story!

Dinner prompt:
- [ ] Think of a time someone said something especially stupid or insulting to you. Write a story in which you respond to that person in the manner you wished to at that time, but likely did not.

Day 259
Five-minute prompt:
☐ Cheer
Midday prompt:
☐ In many cultures, it is believed that a person's name holds power over the person themselves.

Write a story about a woman who has lost her name.
Dinner prompt:
☐ A rich man loses everything - his wife, his home, his job, most of his savings - in the span of a couple of months. He is convinced that he is cursed, and goes to a famous esoteric for help.

By the end of the session, the man has annoyed the person running it so badly that if he weren't cursed before, he sure is now.

Day 260
Five-minute prompt:
- [ ] Evanescence

Midday prompt:
- [ ] A large, orange tomcat plays while his owner attempts to study for her nursing exams.

Dinner prompt:
- [ ] A mother of two feels like a single parent to three unruly kids when her husband joins in on the whining.

Day 261
Five-minute prompt:
- [ ] Burrow

Midday prompt:
- [ ] After months of silent suffering, a man tells off his mean, inconsiderate, and very muscled coworker.

    Said coworker promptly breaks down into tears.

Dinner prompt:
- [ ] A nice, silly dog turns vicious whenever its owner's boyfriend is around.

Day 262

Five-minute prompt:
- ☐ Embrace

Midday prompt:
- ☐ A little girl finds a frog in her locker at school.

Dinner prompt:
- ☐ While on a tour of a Victorian-era home, a man falls through a painting into a secret room.

Day 263

Five-minute prompt:
- ☐ Bound

Midday prompt:
- ☐ A little boy drinks his mother's cup of coffee while she is not paying attention.

Dinner prompt:
- ☐ Something magical happens on a lazy, rain-drenched afternoon.

Day 264
Five-minute prompt:
- [ ] Bubble

Midday prompt:
- [ ] Pick two characters from your previous works; the more dissimilar in nature, the better. Put them in the following situations and describe their reactions.

  - In a long line at the Post Office, with only one clerk working in the front
  - At a birthday party of a person they do not particularly like
  - During an accidental meeting with their secret crush

Dinner prompt:
- [ ] Find an old story of yours - the older, the better. Edit and/or rewrite it.

  Has your writing style changed with time? How drastically?

Day 265
Five-minute prompt:
☐ Hurry

Midday prompt:
☐ A girl finds a hand-written poem tucked between the pages of a book on Advanced Biology she borrows from the school's library. She reads it out-loud, charmed by the silly rhymes.

It turns out the poem is not a poem, but a spell.

Dinner prompt:
☐ A terrible accident leaves a man missing some of his memories. The memory-loss seems limited to a point far in the past, so the man mostly goes on with his life.

That is until a teenage girl shows up at his house, claiming that she is his daughter. The man has no recollection of the girl or the woman she says is her mother.

Day 266

Five-minute prompt:
- Patchwork

Midday prompt:
- Time-capsule challenge!
 Write down five things that you would like to have accomplished in the next five years on a loose sheet of paper. Fold the paper and put it into a glass jar or bottle. Bury it in your backyard (or somewhere you can access in the future).

Dinner prompt:
- Write a story about wrapped perceptions: A character (or a group of characters, or an entire society) sees something one way, when the reality is completely different.

Day 267
Five-minute prompt:
- [ ] Yarn

Midday prompt:
- [ ] A boy does something really stupid to impress a girl he likes. He ends up with a broken arm, but hey - at least she noticed him!

Dinner prompt:
- [ ] While walking back home, a young girl is approached by an old woman. The woman can barely walk, and she asks for the young girl's assistance in getting back to her home a block down the street. The girl is a bit apprehensive, but helps the woman nonetheless.

  Everything is fine, until they reach the old woman's house.

Day 268
Five-minute prompt:
- [ ] Wealth

Midday prompt:
- [ ] A man stumbles upon a garden in full bloom. Atop a mountain. In the middle of winter.

Dinner prompt:
- [ ] A boy suddenly grows bunny ears. High school gets a lot more embarrassing.

Day 269
Five-minute prompt:
- [ ] Heavy

Midday prompt:
- [ ] Re-imagine the ending of a fairy tale. What if one of Cinderella's sisters had married the Prince? How about if Snow White had not been spared by the Huntsman?

Dinner prompt:
- [ ] It has been proposed that people's fear of death is partially motivated by our fear of the unknown.

  Write of a world where everyone knows what happens after a person dies. How is death regarded in this world?

Day 270

Five-minute prompt:
- [ ] Grease

Midday prompt:
- [ ] A man who fears heights gains the ability to fly.

Dinner prompt:
- [ ] In Heian period Japan, women scorned or wronged by their lovers would at times take Buddhist vows and retire to a monastery, usually in a mountain and thus far away from civilization. As the vows included an oath of celibacy and the shaving of one's head, swearing to a life as a nun served as the woman's ultimate denouncement of her beau. Write a story about one such woman.

Day 271
Five-minute prompt:
☐ Fog

Midday prompt:
☐ The members of a popular boy band are forced to split up when several of them file a lawsuit against their management company. Although they are all close friends, part of the band chooses to remain with the company while the rest decide to leave it. Write of the days leading to the decision to file the lawsuit, and its aftermath.

Dinner prompt:
☐ The temperature in one of the rooms in a certain family's home is always drastically different than that of the rest of the house. The family often jokes that the room must contain a door to a different dimension. Turns out, they are right.

Day 272
Five-minute prompt:
- ☐ Edge

Midday prompt:
- ☐ After her village is razed to the ground on the orders of a greedy and merciless King, a woman makes a deal with the Devil in order to get revenge.

Dinner prompt:
- ☐ A couple wins an all-expenses paid trip to an exotic island. The place is gorgeous, the accommodations - extravagant, and the couple falls in love with it all right away. Until night falls and the man-eating creatures native to the island emerge, that is.

Day 273
Five-minute prompt:
- ☐ Chimney

Midday prompt:
- ☐ A woman receives a strange package. It is entirely black and has no label or a return address.

  She opens it.

Dinner prompt:
- ☐ An annoying door-to-door salesman tries to harangue his way into a person's home.

Day 274
Five-minute prompt:
- Letter

Midday prompt:
- Two twenty-something intellectual-wannabes are discussing "things of importance" in loud voices while riding on a crowded public train. A woman on her way back from work sits near the duo, trying to ignore them.

Dinner prompt:
- A woman suffers from terrible nightmares. Her dreams turn out to be prophetic.

Day 275
Five-minute prompt:
- Dance

Midday prompt:
- Two good friends compete against each other for the affections of the same girl. Said girl does not particularly like either of them.

Dinner prompt:
- A man says something hurtful to a person dear to him. He regrets it immediately but words, once spoken, cannot be taken back.

Day 276

Five-minute prompt:
- ☐ Salute

Midday prompt:
- ☐ Cool-kid wannabe's grandmother friends him on his social media account.

Dinner prompt:
- ☐ A grouchy, single, middle-aged man gets saddled with his sister's children over a long weekend.

Day 277

Five-minute prompt:
- ☐ Corridor

Midday prompt:
- ☐ A sales representative at a high-scale cosmetics store is torn between honesty and the desire to make a sale as she watches a customer load her cart with expensive, but absolutely unsuitable make-up products.

Dinner prompt:
- ☐ A drunk man stumbling home late at night wonders if he is seeing things, or if there really is a cat sporting a top-hat lounging on his front steps.

Day 278
Five-minute prompt:
- [ ] Foul

Midday prompt:
- [ ] Two young children - a boy and a girl - are out trick-or-treating with their parents for the first time. At a particularly well-decorated house, an automated witch scares the little boy into crying. His sister promptly takes action.

Dinner prompt:
- [ ] Two housewives with neighboring houses have a passive-aggressive battle involving baked goods, yard sales, and increasingly extravagant home decorations.

Day 279
Five-minute prompt:
☐ Blemish
Midday prompt:
☐ A poet is forced to take a job writing songs for pop-stars at an entertainment company. He submits quality work, but more often than not has his lyrics revised or completely rejected. In a fit of anger, the poet writes a song filled with the corniest, most trite lines he can think of.

It is an unimagined success.
Dinner prompt:
☐ A man grows up hearing rumors about a strange woman living alone deep in the forests of a nearby mountain. Some call her a witch; others dismiss her as unsound of mind. The man decides to find out if the woman exists and if so, if the stories about her hold any truth.

Day 280
Five-minute prompt:
- [ ] Dust

Midday prompt:
- [ ] A little boy slips and falls from a bridge into a deep lake.

  He is saved by a kind, if a bit strange creature.

Dinner prompt:
- [ ] Two sisters spend their summer vacation at their grandmother's house. Soon, they notice something strange: There is always a light on in the attic at night, even though their grandmother never goes up there.

  They decide to investigate.

Day 281
Five-minute prompt:
- ☐ Lace

Midday prompt:
- ☐ A girl is gifted with a beautiful doll. Soon, the girl notices something strange: The doll's hair seems to be getting longer...

Dinner prompt:
- ☐ Two lions lounge atop the warm rocks in their cramped zoo enclosure, planning on how to get to the annoying people waving and shouting at them but feet away.

Day 282
Five-minute prompt:
- ☐ Dress

Midday prompt:
- ☐ Long hours and an unforgiving profession has led a man to drift away from his family. When he realizes that he has not spoken a single word to his children in over a week, the man decides he has had enough and quits his job.

Dinner prompt:
- ☐ Two tiny faeries sneak into a child's bedroom, meaning to spirit her away.
  The child's pet poodle is having none of it.

Day 283
Five-minute prompt:
- [ ] Mask

Midday prompt:
- [ ] A rooster has an encounter with a vegetarian fox.

Dinner prompt:
- [ ] A couple who can no longer stand each other go to a marriage counselor.

Day 284
Five-minute prompt:
- [ ] Tourniquet

Midday prompt:
- [ ] Describe a day in the life of a young woman living in a dangerous neighborhood.

Dinner prompt:
- [ ] Unable to find a job after graduating college, a brilliant young man/woman finally succumbs to the need for money and takes a menial job at a local supermarket. He/she expects a boring, if physically demanding days and is not at all prepared for the work-drama that awaits.

Day 285
Five-minute prompt:
- ☐ Petal

Midday prompt:
- ☐ What is meant to be a relaxing day out fishing turns hilariously disastrous as a group of children stumble upon a man's fishing spot and proceed to bug both him and the local wildlife.

Dinner prompt:
- ☐ Write a story that is as concise as possible. Once you have written it, look over the story again and eliminate any words or sentences that are extraneous. Strive for the simplest, most direct tale you can manage.

Day 286
Five-minute prompt:
- ☐ Cherry

Midday prompt:
- ☐ A man who has the ability to see the future foresees his child's murder.

  He recognizes the person responsible, as well.

Dinner prompt:
- ☐ A moody teenager goes shopping with her mother.

Day 287

Five-minute prompt:
- [ ] Hunger

Midday prompt:
- [ ] Two sets of grandparents fight over the name of their newborn grandchild. Each wants the baby named after someone in their family. Tired and exasperated, the baby's mother names her child after her favorite book character and tells everyone to get out.

Dinner prompt:
- [ ] A teen has taken to talking in text-lingo. His/her parents can no longer understand a word he/she is saying.

Day 288

Five-minute prompt:
- [ ] Drone

Midday prompt:
- [ ] Write a story that begins with its end.

Dinner prompt:
- [ ] A man who is direct and honest by nature finds himself in a work environment where slyness and subtle cattiness are the norm in office interactions.

Day 289

Five-minute prompt:
- [ ] Teem

Midday prompt:
- [ ] Write a story that begins and ends with the same sentence.

Dinner prompt:
- [ ] Standing by a friend during a difficult time in their lives is glorified by society. But what if doing so is harmful for the person doing the "standing?"

Write a story in which a person breaks contact with a friend in need in order to save their own sanity and nerves.

Day 290

Five-minute prompt:
- [ ] Kite

Midday prompt:
- [ ] Is there a challenge or an obstacle that you are currently facing? Brainstorm ideas for alleviating or eliminating the difficulty altogether.

Dinner prompt:
- [ ] A meteor collides with Earth. In addition to the widespread damage and enormous loss of life, clouds of dust have risen in the atmosphere, plunging the planet in darkness. A year after the incident, survivors have somewhat adapted to their new, darker lives. That is when strange beings start to emerge from within the dark skies...

Day 291

Five-minute prompt:
- [ ] Soar

Midday prompt:
- [ ] A naive, romantic man finds himself charmed beyond reason by a sarcastic, pessimistic woman.

   Let the courting commence!

Dinner prompt:
- [ ] A man buys the bulldog he has always wanted while his wife is away on a business trip. And a cat. And a parrot.

Day 292

Five-minute prompt:
- [ ] Conscious

Midday prompt:
- [ ] A girl finds her mother's old diary.

Dinner prompt:
- [ ] A man buys an owl and trains it to carry letters.

   People really, really hate getting mail from him.

Day 293
Five-minute prompt:
- Metal

Midday prompt:
- A naturally timid person is put in a situation in which being aggressive is the only way to go.

Dinner prompt:
- Write a how-to guide regarding the proper use of an iron (for ironing clothes). Explain in steps, with as much detail as possible. Assume that a potential reader knows nothing of operating irons - or even what they are!

Day 294

Five-minute prompt:

☐ Cuff

Midday prompt:

☐ A merchant is traveling through a forest on his way to a town in which he plans to sell his wares. He chances upon a small pond; thirsty, he halts his horse and unsaddles. Water-jug in hand, he kneels by the pond.
Freezes.
There is something staring up at him from within the lake's depths.

Dinner prompt:

☐ A girl dreams a dream she has had many times: A nightmare about a vicious dog that had once belonged to her neighbors. This time, something is different - there is someone else in the dream with her.

Day 295
Five-minute prompt:
- [ ] Toy

Midday prompt:
- [ ] A schoolgirl hires an out-of-work detective to find a lost necklace that had been given to her by her mother.

    He finds it, along with a whole lot of trouble.

Dinner prompt:
- [ ] A mechanic with a gift for writing has secretly been submitting his stories to a small magazine for years.

    When one of his stories is nominated for a Pulitzer Prize, the man finds himself scrutinized by the literary world - and found lacking.

Day 296

Five-minute prompt:
- [ ] Drum

Midday prompt:
- [ ] In Greek mythology, there exist beings by the name of "Furies:" terrifying female demigods who take vengeance upon mortals guilty of terrible crimes.

   Write about a man haunted by a Fury.

Dinner prompt:
- [ ] A woman falls asleep in her office at work. When she wakes up, she finds that she is alone, the office is dark, and all the doors are locked. Knowing that she has no excuse about missing the punch-out time and not particularly eager to be fired for sleeping on the job, the woman decides to spend the night there instead of calling for help.

   She finds quite a bit to occupy her time, especially in the files kept in her boss' office.

Day 297

Five-minute prompt:
- [ ] Collar

Midday prompt:
- [ ] A boy finds out his mother had been an actress after purchasing an old VHS tape from a local rental store that's going out of business.

Dinner prompt:
- [ ] Every year on her birthday, a girl obsessed with fantasy books wishes for something magical to happen to her.

    On her twenty-first birthday, her wish finally comes true.

Day 298
Five-minute prompt:
- ☐ Remote

Midday prompt:
- ☐ A man grows horns. And then a tail. Wings, too.
  He really wishes that people would stop screaming and pointing.

Dinner prompt:
- ☐ A merciless, sardonic, and generally unpleasant man finds himself the romantic interest of a peppy high school teacher who recently moved in next door.

Day 299
Five-minute prompt:
- ☐ Still

Midday prompt:
- ☐ Write a story that reads like a dream: Convoluted, vivid, seemingly logical yet saying nothing at all in the end.

Dinner prompt:
- ☐ A woman who no longer believes in anything witnesses a miracle.

Day 300
Five-minute prompt:
- [ ] Intricate

Midday prompt:
- [ ] Write a story around a character that fits one of the sixteen personality types described on the website below.

    Full link:
    http://www.16personalities.com/personality-types.

    You are also welcome to Google-search "personality types" and find a site that you like.

Dinner prompt:
- [ ] A man fresh out of college decides to go backpacking across Europe.
    A day into the journey, he realizes that his idea of what travelling abroad entails differs greatly from the reality.

Day 301

Five-minute prompt:
☐ Wooden

Midday prompt:
☐ A man forgets his suitcase on the train while traveling home from work. Thankfully, he remembers it in time and is able to hail the conductor and retrieve it.

When he gets back home, the man realizes he must have the wrong suitcase, as his was definitely not filled with neat stacks of money.

Dinner prompt:
☐ An evil wizard is transformed into a kitten, courtesy of a failed spell meant to bring doom to his enemies.

Ignorant of what had happened, one of said enemies decides to take the wizard-turned-kitten for her pet.

Day 302
Five-minute prompt:
- [ ] Willow

Midday prompt:
- [ ] A girl confesses her love to a boy, only to have her feelings thrown in her face. Ten years later, the man said boy has become finds himself unknowingly pursuing that same girl.

Dinner prompt:
- [ ] Below, you will find three examples of literary devices writers use to enrich their writing. Use each of them in a sentence.

    - *Alliteration*: the repetition of initial consonant sounds, often in consecutive words. Ex: beastly beauty.
    - *Epizeuxis*: the repetition of a single word, for emphasis. Ex: Living in the countryside is dull, dull, dull.
    - *Pleonasm:* using more words than necessary in order to make a point. Ex: I saw it with my own eyes.

Day 303
Five-minute prompt:
- ☐ Translucent

Midday prompt:
- ☐ A little white lie snowballs into a great big problem.

Dinner prompt:
- ☐ Have you done something that you later regretted? What was it? Looking back on the situation now, do you believe you could have - or should have - acted in a different way?

Day 304
Five-minute prompt:
- ☐ Crescent

Midday prompt:
- ☐ Working the night-shift has turned a woman nocturnal: She sleeps during the day and stays up all night, regardless of whether it is a work day or the weekend. The change of lifestyle does not bother the woman too much. Her neighbor, on the other hand, is convinced she has become a vampire.

Dinner prompt:
- ☐ A man forgets his son at the supermarket. He remembers half-way home and drives frantically back, only to find--

Day 305
Five-minute prompt:
- Gamble

Midday prompt:
- A girl's father is really enthusiastic about technology, despite being absolutely dreadful at using it. He buys the newest smart-phone available on the market, and then proceeds to bug his daughter with questions.

Dinner prompt:
- An extremely clumsy man accidentally stops a would-be robbery by tripping over the bad guy.

Day 306
Five-minute prompt:
- Ominous

Midday prompt:
- Write a story from second-person point of view.

Dinner prompt:
- Check today's horoscope for a zodiac sign of your choice. Write a story around a character of that sign who has a day exactly as foretold by his/her horoscope.

Day 307

Five-minute prompt:
- [ ] Herd

Midday prompt:
- [ ] Unrest in their native lands forces an alien princess and her family to emigrate to Earth. The girl is about fifteen Earth years old, and not too thrilled about attending a human school.

    Especially since no one on Earth even knows of her planet's existence.

Dinner prompt:
- [ ] In German lore, there exists a "Christmas demon" by the name of Krampus. On Christmas Eve, Krampus accompanies Father Christmas and punishes the children who have been bad, while St. Nicholas leaves gifts for those who have been good. Krampus is commonly depicted as carrying a bundle of birch sticks, rattling long chains, and generally looking very devil-like.

    Write a story about a boy who has misbehaved during the year, and thus encounters Krampus on Christmas Eve.

Day 308
Five-minute prompt:
- [ ] Coalescent

Midday prompt:
- [ ] In a world where people are born with the date of their death written on their bodies, a woman falls in love with a man that has a year and a day left to live.

Dinner prompt:
- [ ] Write a story in which you deliberately ignore grammatical rules. Try to create certain feelings and effects by doing so, rather than simply writing erroneously.

Day 309
Five-minute prompt:
- [ ] Holy

Midday prompt:
- [ ] Write a story about the same one hour in the day of three people. You will end up with three stories in one, the only connection being the time during which each is occurring.

Dinner prompt:
- [ ] A girl in white counts crows upon a frozen field.

Day 310

Five-minute prompt:
- [ ] Prayer

Midday prompt:
- [ ] A thief steals a cursed statue. As his luck takes a turn for the worst, he tries to return the statue.

The previous owner proves to be a problem.

Dinner prompt:
- [ ] A lonely man finds solace in the most unexpected place.

Day 311

Five-minute prompt:
- [ ] Weight

Midday prompt:
- [ ] A man falls ill with a strange sickness. He begins to sleep more and more, his dreams grow as vivid as reality, until he can no longer separate reality from fiction.

Dinner prompt:
- [ ] Write a story with an ambiguous end.

Day 312
Five-minute prompt:
- [ ] Frozen

Midday prompt:
- [ ] A girl writes a fanfiction featuring her favorite actor.
  Said actor reads it and comments about the story on live TV.

Dinner prompt:
- [ ] A sleep-over turns strange when people begin to disappear... only to return, not seeming like themselves.

Day 313
Five-minute prompt:
- [ ] Star

Midday prompt:
- [ ] A boy wakes up to see flickering lights by his bedroom window.

Dinner prompt:
- [ ] In a slowly dying world, a young man cares for his ailing friend. The two are the last remaining survivors of the human race.

Day 314
Five-minute prompt:
☐ Bay
Midday prompt:
☐ A landslide leaves a group of hikers stranded in a mountainous region during a terrible storm.
Dinner prompt:
☐ The night of the first day of the new year, an anthropologist witnesses a strange dance performed by a group of people in the center of a rural village. Curious, she asks the villagers about the dance and whether it holds any cultural significance.

The villagers have no idea what she is talking about.

Day 315
Five-minute prompt:
☐ Wire
Midday prompt:
☐ A man finds a fox cub in his gardens. It appears sick, so he brings it home and attempts to heal it.
Dinner prompt:
☐ Write a story which occurs in the span of ten seconds.

Day 316
Five-minute prompt:
- [ ] Worm

Midday prompt:
- [ ] A noble is banished to the outskirts of the kingdom after he commits a small transgression at Court. Initially angry at his dismissal from the Capital, the noble soon finds himself warming up to the provincial town he has been tasked to administer.

Dinner prompt:
- [ ] Record something that has happened to you as a historian would a past event. Try to be as objective as possible.

Day 317

Five-minute prompt:
- [ ] Rosary

Midday prompt:
- [ ] Think of as many synonyms of (or alternatives to) the following words, as they would be used in a story:
    - Say
    - Beautiful
    - Angry
    - Smile

Dinner prompt:
- [ ] One afternoon, a woman returns home to find her husband gone - along with all of his possessions. Heartbroken, she assumes that he has left her.

    Five years later, she discovers something that has her rethinking the whole accident.

Day 318
Five-minute prompt:
- [ ] Power

Midday prompt:
- [ ] A teenager overhears his mother complaining about him/her to her best friend.
  At first, the teen feels angry; then he/she realizes his/her mother is right.

Dinner prompt:
- [ ] A set of fraternal twins, a boy and a girl, look and act astonishingly alike. So much so that their friends at times make embarrassing mistakes...

Day 319
Five-minute prompt:
- [ ] Spell

Midday prompt:
- [ ] Capture a single moment of extraordinary emotion in a story.

Dinner prompt:
- [ ] A man heavily in debt to a shady underground organization attempts to escape gangsters and corrupt cops as he tries to figure out a way to return the money - and keep his life.

Day 320
Five-minute prompt:
- [ ] Soul

Midday prompt:
- [ ] Write a story that begins as follows: Two people walk along a long, empty road.

Dinner prompt:
- [ ] A pair of high school sweethearts grows up and grows apart.

Day 321
Five-minute prompt:
- [ ] Lipstick

Midday prompt:
- [ ] A retired superhero is forced to pick up the mantle once again when her children are threatened.

Dinner prompt:
- [ ] Write a story inspired by the following line: "The revolution is in your mind."

Day 322

Five-minute prompt:

- [ ] Luminescent

Midday prompt:

- [ ] Describe a world of magic.

Dinner prompt:

- [ ] A girl falls through a crack in time into a dimension identical to ours, with the exception of it not being inhabited by living beings.

Day 323

Five-minute prompt:

- [ ] Peppermint

Midday prompt:

- [ ] A famous boxer is forced from the ring for the sake of his health. At loose ends and in the possession of too much built-up aggression, he decides to join a knitting club. It proves to be much less relaxing than advertised.

Dinner prompt:

- [ ] A little girl grooms her pet dog. The poor dog finds itself sporting a feathered hat, clip-on earrings, and curling rolls in its fur.

Day 324
Five-minute prompt:
- ☐ Hornet

Midday prompt:
- ☐ Write a short story set in a specific historical period. Focus on the setting, the clothing of your characters, and their manner of speaking.

Dinner prompt:
- ☐ At a party, a woman kisses a frog someone found on a dare.
    It turns into a prince.

Day 325
Five-minute prompt:
- ☐ Fur

Midday prompt:
- ☐ A family moves into a house infested with...bunnies?

Dinner prompt:
- ☐ A teenage boy writes awful poems dedicated to his crush. He never meant for her to find out about them, though.

Day 326
Five-minute prompt:
- Hue

Midday prompt:
- A timid girl finds herself caught between her two best friends when they have a falling out. Driven to the end of her patience, she gives them both a piece of her mind - and scares them right back into a friendship.

Dinner prompt:
- Evaluate the following saying:
  There is no good without evil, and no evil without good.

Day 327
Five-minute prompt:
- Bush

Midday prompt:
- Write a story set in the Wild West. Feature a cowboy who cannot shoot a gun and a woman meant to be a love interest who cannot care less about romance.

Dinner prompt:
- A girl is dragged into an adventure quite against her will.

Day 328

Five-minute prompt:

☐ Zealous

Midday prompt:

☐ A man fixes up his grandfather's old typewriter. Eager to try writing on it, he loads the typewriter with a new sheet of paper; however, a phone call distracts him and he forgets all about it.

The following day, the man goes back to the typewriter. All is as he has left it - with the exception of the sheet of paper, which is filled from top to bottom with neatly-typed words.

Dinner prompt:

☐ A girl introduces her father to her imaginary friend.

Said friend is not exactly imaginary.

Day 329
Five-minute prompt:
- [ ] Bow

Midday prompt:
- [ ] An old woman recounts the greatest triumphs in her life.

Dinner prompt:
- [ ] A man loses the love of his life, before he ever has a chance to tell her know how he feels.

    A chance encounter with a magical creature gives him an unexpected second chance.

Day 330
Five-minute prompt:
- [ ] Ink

Midday prompt:
- [ ] A celebrity goes to his/her high school reunion, mostly out of spite. High school was not the best time of his/her life, and he/she is eager to show off a bit.

Dinner prompt:
- [ ] After pissing off the wrong person, a man is transfigured into a woman for one month. In other words, he is literally forced to walk into someone else's shoes.

Day 331

Five-minute prompt:
- ☐ Ranger

Midday prompt:
- ☐ A warrior thinks about the things that rule his life: Battle, King, and family. He realizes he only cares about one of them.

Dinner prompt:
- ☐ Historically, astronomers were often employed by the ruling nobility. They read the stars in order to foretell coming events of importance, such as wars, draughts, or famines.
  Write a story that features such an astronomer, and a forthcoming disaster.

Day 332

Five-minute prompt:
- ☐ Imp

Midday prompt:
- ☐ A troll visits a human village.

Dinner prompt:
- ☐ If you could relive a day in your past, which day would it be? Why?

Day 333
Five-minute prompt:
- ☐ Resurrection

Midday prompt:
- ☐ A girl visits the future. It is nothing she would have ever expected.

Dinner prompt:
- ☐ Look outside. Select one object - be it a tree, a house, a car, a person - and write a story around them. Describe the object in as great detail as possible, while avoiding clichés.

Day 334
Five-minute prompt:
- ☐ Songbird

Midday prompt:
- ☐ While clearing out her family's basement, a woman finds a picture album that belonged to her grandmother.

Dinner prompt:
- ☐ A strange flower has bloomed in a neighborhood garden. Its petals are pitch-black, its leaves large and blue-green, and its aroma has people seeing bizarre things indeed.

Day 335
Five-minute prompt:
- [ ] Wave

Midday prompt:
- [ ] Do you have a pet-peeve? What is it? How do you deal with it, when you encounter it?

Dinner prompt:
- [ ] A boy is studying to be a botanist. His father, a retired Army Colonel, is not too pleased.

Day 336
Five-minute prompt:
- [ ] Mermaid

Midday prompt:
- [ ] A man frustrated with his marriage signs up for a dating site. He feels drawn to a woman he meets there, and starts developing feelings for her.

  The woman, as it turns out, is far from a stranger.

Dinner prompt:
- [ ] A demon complains to an angel about his job.

Day 337
Five-minute prompt:
☐ Wish

Midday prompt:
☐ In literature, a tragic flaw is a trait in the protagonist of a tragedy that eventually causes their ruin. Write a story featuring a protagonist who possesses a tragic flaw.

Dinner prompt:
☐ Early morning by the sea. An old fisherman sits on a deserted beach, patching up a long coil of fishing nets.

Suddenly, a figure emerges from the sea. It walks up to the fisherman and sits beside him.

Day 338

Five-minute prompt:

☐ Rome

Midday prompt:

☐ Hans Christian Andersen's beautiful fairy-tale, "The Snow Queen," begins with the breaking of the Devil's mirror - a large, ghastly thing that twists whatever is reflected in it to appear ugly and wrong. Pieces of the mirror are carried all over the world, entering people's eyes and bodies and wrapping their perceptions of reality.

Write a story of someone who has inadvertently swallowed a piece of the Devil's mirror.

Dinner prompt:

☐ A woman loses everything she thought she wanted, only to find herself with everything she actually needs.

Day 339
Five-minute prompt:
- [ ] Needle

Midday prompt:
- [ ] A man gains perspective after an accident at work leaves him with a temporary loss of sight.

Dinner prompt:
- [ ] After a shipwreck, a man finds himself stranded on a remote and unpopulated island. What's worse, the only other survivor of the wreck appears to be his ex-wife.

Day 340
Five-minute prompt:
- [ ] Straw

Midday prompt:
- [ ] A girl meets an online friend for the first time. Only they turn out to be...not exactly human.

Dinner prompt:
- [ ] Tell a story about a cloud.

Day 341
Five-minute prompt:
- ☐ Yowl

Midday prompt:
- ☐ A man finds the end of the rainbow. What is on the other side?

Dinner prompt:
- ☐ A hot summer day in a small, boring town. A teen is smoking behind a school. Suddenly--

---

Day 342
Five-minute prompt:
- ☐ Window

Midday prompt:
- ☐ A girl meets a dust fairy that lives beneath her bed.

Dinner prompt:
- ☐ Personify the days of the week. Write a story that has them interacting with each other.

Day 343
Five-minute prompt:
☐ Pumpkin

Midday prompt:
☐ Write a story that is told hour-by-hour, with every hour in a single day mentioned.

Dinner prompt:
☐ Has something made you disillusioned with the world, however briefly?

Day 344
Five-minute prompt:
☐ Seed

Midday prompt:
☐ Two farmers talk about the drought that has befallen their country. One is superstitious, and believes the draught to have a supernatural cause; the other is realistic and points to more logical reasons for the lack of rain.

Dinner prompt:
☐ A boy discovers that a single smile is at times enough to make one's day better.

Day 345

Five-minute prompt:
☐ Morale

Midday prompt:
☐ True strength is in the mind.
Write a story in which a strong man is pitted against a smart man, and loses.

Dinner prompt:
☐ A woman lives in a fantasy world of her own making; she immerses herself in books and movies, ignoring or wrapping the reality around her.
As a result, she is quite unprepared to face the real world and its less-than-nice inhabitants once she leaves the safety of college.

Day 346
Five-minute prompt:
☐ Scorched
Midday prompt:
☐ Write about an absolutely lazy day, where nothing of note happens but everything is wonderful anyway.
Dinner prompt:
☐ After a storm destroys their home, a family discovers a treasure buried in the house's foundation.

Every evil for good, people say.

Day 347
Five-minute prompt:
☐ Foil
Midday prompt:
☐ After work, a woman boards the train she usually takes home. Her car is almost empty, which strikes her a bit strange - it is six o'clock in the afternoon, well into rush hour. She shrugs it off to luck and sets to reading her book.

When the train makes its first stop, however, the woman realizes something is wrong. The stop is not one she is familiar with - or indeed, that should exist in reality at all.

Dinner prompt:
☐ A visiting opera gains fame when one of its actors dies on stage, during a live performance. What is more, the cause of death is by no means natural.

Day 348
Five-minute prompt:
- [ ] Tail

Midday prompt:
- [ ] Two little girls break their mother's collection of glass elephants while playing. Their mother sits them down and explains the importance of respecting what other people hold dear.

Dinner prompt:
- [ ] Write a story that centers around numbers.

Day 349
Five-minute prompt:
- [ ] Hymn

Midday prompt:
- [ ] In a world on the verge of destruction, a scientist accidentally discovers time travel.

Dinner prompt:
- [ ] A girl fights off a very real monster with nothing but kindness.

Day 350
Five-minute prompt:
- Arch

Midday prompt:
- Write a story of a self-made man. Make sure to include his views on the world and his fellow people.

Dinner prompt:
- Pick a song at random. Write a story while listening to it. Write only as long as the song lasts - not a word beyond the last second!

Day 351
Five-minute prompt:
- Coral

Midday prompt:
- Write of a world where everything exists in extremes. There is nothing uncertain and nothing in-between; everything is either one way or another. Evil is evil, good is good, love is fanatical and hate - all-encompassing.

Dinner prompt:
- Apollo, the Greek god of music, truth, and prophecy, falls in love with a human promised to the god of war, Ares.

Day 352
Five-minute prompt:
- [ ] Jagged

Midday prompt:
- [ ] A warrior takes a beautiful sword as spoils of his most recent military success.
  The sword is haunted by the ghost of a man the warrior killed during battle.

Dinner prompt:
- [ ] Write a story of betrayal.

Day 353
Five-minute prompt:
- [ ] Hunt

Midday prompt:
- [ ] A spirit attaches itself to a woman and wrecks havoc in her life. After a consultation with a medium, the woman learns that the only way to get rid of the specter is to find the person responsible for its death.

Dinner prompt:
- [ ] Write a short story by hand, using your non-dominant hand.
  Do you find yourself thinking more before writing?

Day 354

Five-minute prompt:
- [ ] Jungle

Midday prompt:
- [ ] A boy becomes an adult in the span of a day.

Dinner prompt:
- [ ] A girl discovers she has a fairy-godmother. A very quirky, possibly insane fairy-godmother.

Day 355

Five-minute prompt:
- [ ] Concrete

Midday prompt:
- [ ] Write about a birthday celebration that involves bad presents, exploding cake, and accidental intoxication.

Dinner prompt:
- [ ] A delivery girl is sent to deliver a pizza to the house of her crush. Initially embarrassed, she decides to suck it up and do her job. She is not at all prepared for the awkward, star-struck way in which her crush reacts upon seeing her at his door.

Day 356
Five-minute prompt:
- [ ] Dante

Midday prompt:
- [ ] Write a story in which an apparent injustice is explained and given reason.

Dinner prompt:
- [ ] Two kids plan an adorable, loving Mother's Day for their hardworking mom.

Day 357
Five-minute prompt:
- [ ] Woven

Midday prompt:
- [ ] A man who has long ago given up on his dreams has his dearest wish literally fall into his lap.

Dinner prompt:
- [ ] Two soldiers of opposing armies experience a surreal time of truce when a terrible earthquake collapses part of the battlefield, trapping the men in an underground cavern.

Day 358

Five-minute prompt:
- ☐ Regret

Midday prompt:
- ☐ A woman plays a game of chance against the Devil.

Dinner prompt:
- ☐ A man finds a strange music box that plays different tunes depending on the mood of the person who opens it.

Day 359

Five-minute prompt:
- ☐ Justice

Midday prompt:
- ☐ A woman meets her idol, and finds him lacking.

Dinner prompt:
- ☐ A goat herder teaches a scholar something about life that is not taught in books.

Day 360

Five-minute prompt:
- [ ] Tyranny

Midday prompt:
- [ ] A little girl believes that her next-door neighbor is a wizard.
  Despite what her parents think, she is not actually wrong.

Dinner prompt:
- [ ] Write a story that includes the sound of rain.

Day 361

Five-minute prompt:
- [ ] Jasmine

Midday prompt:
- [ ] A man finds a letter by his front door. It is addressed to him, but bears no stamp or a return address. He opens it. The very first word gives him pause; it reads, "Dad." The man has no children.

Dinner prompt:
- [ ] Write a story that will make the reader smile.

Day 362

Five-minute prompt:
- [ ] Trope

Midday prompt:
- [ ] Following his parents' death, a young boy finds himself bumped from relative to relative, with no stable home or loving care to be found.

   After a year of such misfortune, he is suddenly adopted by a mysterious uncle he had never previously met. The man is rich and extremely kind to the boy.

   He is also a bit magic.

Dinner prompt:
- [ ] A man and a woman marry against their respective families' wishes. Consequently, no one turns up for their wedding.

   The couple finds it hard to care, happy as they are.

Day 363
Five-minute prompt:
- Empire

Midday prompt:
- An ailing King chooses to give his kingdom to his youngest son, bypassing his elder brother. The scorned son is enraged and hatches a plan to kill his brother and gain the crown.

Dinner prompt:
- Write a story featuring a character who continuously makes bad puns and tawdry jokes.

Day 364
Five-minute prompt:
- Gargoyle

Midday prompt:
- Pick a current news topic and write a newspaper report on it. Style it as a parody.

Dinner prompt:
- A bad cold has a girl losing her voice. Forced to be silent, she learns a lot about her friends and family.

Day 365

Five-minute prompt:

☐ Instant

Midday prompt:

☐ A girl makes an embarrassing music video as a joke. Her little brother posts it online without her knowledge.

By the next morning, she is internet-famous.

Dinner prompt:

☐ A man discovers that a family of foxes has made a home beneath his house.

Day 366

Five-minute prompt:

☐ Mutiny

Midday prompt:

☐ Create a Coat of Arms for your family, including a family slogan to go along with it.

Dinner prompt:

☐ A sinner walks into a place of worship late at night.

Morning Fives

Write whatever comes to mind. Write for five minutes or so; do not pause to edit! Disconnected, disjointed, disorientated - it's all good!

☐	Peaches	☐	Thunder
☐	Circlet	☐	Earl
☐	Smudged	☐	Ash
☐	Fall	☐	Sear
☐	Grasp	☐	Soothe
☐	Fair	☐	Amber
☐	Salt	☐	Dimple
☐	Grain	☐	Goodbye
☐	Hour	☐	Callous
☐	Crumpled	☐	Tiara
☐	Tumble	☐	Arrow
☐	Spill	☐	Bone
☐	Bullet	☐	Bite
☐	Flesh	☐	Full
☐	Moonrise	☐	Legion
☐	Asunder	☐	Caravan
☐	Myth	☐	Beast
☐	Tart	☐	Treacherous
☐	Ravine	☐	Shadow
☐	Stilted	☐	Silhouette
☐	Facade	☐	Fruit

- ☐ Sin
- ☐ Crown
- ☐ Thorn
- ☐ Forsaken
- ☐ Guilt
- ☐ Rouge
- ☐ Stone
- ☐ Crystal
- ☐ Echo
- ☐ Ego
- ☐ Owl
- ☐ Soft
- ☐ Steel
- ☐ Battle
- ☐ Rim
- ☐ Melancholy
- ☐ Thirst
- ☐ Card
- ☐ Queen
- ☐ Captive
- ☐ Torn
- ☐ Ares
- ☐ Twin
- ☐ Eyes
- ☐ Dog
- ☐ Cross
- ☐ Faith
- ☐ Famine
- ☐ Crocodile
- ☐ Drop
- ☐ Garden
- ☐ Rose
- ☐ Kiss
- ☐ Verbose
- ☐ Golden
- ☐ Rogue
- ☐ Fire
- ☐ Silence
- ☐ Iris
- ☐ Goddess
- ☐ Night
- ☐ Strength
- ☐ Burglar
- ☐ Royal
- ☐ Serenade
- ☐ Malice
- ☐ Tremble
- ☐ Fate
- ☐ Chess
- ☐ Survive
- ☐ Talon
- ☐ Sign
- ☐ Mirror
- ☐ Glaze
- ☐ Barn
- ☐ Curdle
- ☐ Freak
- ☐ Mercy
- ☐ Tear
- ☐ Dirge

A Year of Creative Writing Prompts

- ☐ Cerberus
- ☐ Mortal
- ☐ Trust
- ☐ Triangle
- ☐ Fastidious
- ☐ Dove
- ☐ Sand
- ☐ Solemn
- ☐ Moot
- ☐ Bumble
- ☐ Crumble
- ☐ Smile
- ☐ Balloon
- ☐ Danger
- ☐ Dune
- ☐ Sister
- ☐ Covet
- ☐ Blue
- ☐ Flirt
- ☐ Simper
- ☐ Frost
- ☐ Wine
- ☐ Leader
- ☐ Pest
- ☐ Mime
- ☐ Red
- ☐ Tingle
- ☐ Path
- ☐ Fair
- ☐ Lie
- ☐ Struck
- ☐ Careen
- ☐ Forgotten
- ☐ Tar
- ☐ Fleeting
- ☐ Beach
- ☐ Storm
- ☐ Mars
- ☐ Bitter
- ☐ August
- ☐ Paints
- ☐ Satin
- ☐ Heat
- ☐ Dark
- ☐ Son
- ☐ Shun
- ☐ Greed
- ☐ Bee
- ☐ Sauna
- ☐ Vain
- ☐ Bell
- ☐ Fear
- ☐ Folly
- ☐ Deluge
- ☐ Monotone
- ☐ Bud
- ☐ Tread
- ☐ Forest
- ☐ Tale
- ☐ Sworn

- ☐ Brother
- ☐ Rise
- ☐ Raven
- ☐ Shore
- ☐ Grave
- ☐ Vivid
- ☐ Lily
- ☐ Rambunctious
- ☐ Pretty
- ☐ Silver
- ☐ Horns
- ☐ Stain
- ☐ Pepper
- ☐ Sorrow
- ☐ Spoil
- ☐ Machine
- ☐ Lost
- ☐ Mark
- ☐ Gap
- ☐ Heart
- ☐ Comply
- ☐ Sea
- ☐ Hill
- ☐ Daunting
- ☐ Bundle
- ☐ Corrode
- ☐ Cradle
- ☐ Smoke
- ☐ Sweet
- ☐ Master
- ☐ Misery
- ☐ Rove
- ☐ Headless
- ☐ Crop
- ☐ Vicious
- ☐ Cost
- ☐ Harvest
- ☐ Sly
- ☐ Fruitless
- ☐ Halo
- ☐ Sturdy
- ☐ Lure
- ☐ Spice
- ☐ Creep
- ☐ Corporate
- ☐ Train
- ☐ Island
- ☐ Bridge
- ☐ Song
- ☐ Belief
- ☐ Ship
- ☐ Trudge
- ☐ City
- ☐ Duck
- ☐ Last
- ☐ Loop
- ☐ Hoard
- ☐ Home
- ☐ Statue
- ☐ Shell

A Year of Creative Writing Prompts

- ☐ Hollow
- ☐ Sleepless
- ☐ Stale
- ☐ Possess
- ☐ Simple
- ☐ Sow
- ☐ Human
- ☐ Desert
- ☐ Bustle
- ☐ Enigma
- ☐ Pearl
- ☐ Saddle
- ☐ Compromise
- ☐ Trunk
- ☐ Glass
- ☐ Footstep
- ☐ Fang
- ☐ Cumbersome
- ☐ Cheer
- ☐ Burrow
- ☐ Bubble
- ☐ Hurry
- ☐ Yarn
- ☐ Heavy
- ☐ Fog
- ☐ Chimney
- ☐ Dance
- ☐ Corridor
- ☐ Blemish
- ☐ Lace
- ☐ Dry
- ☐ Chosen
- ☐ Drawn
- ☐ Precious
- ☐ Fairy
- ☐ Stitch
- ☐ Want
- ☐ Dear
- ☐ Circus
- ☐ Teal
- ☐ Sunk
- ☐ Capricious
- ☐ Champion
- ☐ Gramophone
- ☐ Courage
- ☐ Notes
- ☐ Barrel
- ☐ Lacquer
- ☐ Evanescence
- ☐ Embrace
- ☐ Bound
- ☐ Patchwork
- ☐ Wealth
- ☐ Grease
- ☐ Edge
- ☐ Letter
- ☐ Salute
- ☐ Foul
- ☐ Dust
- ☐ Dress

- ☐ Mask
- ☐ Petal
- ☐ Hunger
- ☐ Teem
- ☐ Soar
- ☐ Metal
- ☐ Toy
- ☐ Collar
- ☐ Still
- ☐ Wooden
- ☐ Translucent
- ☐ Gamble
- ☐ Herd
- ☐ Holy
- ☐ Weight
- ☐ Star
- ☐ Wire
- ☐ Rosary
- ☐ Spell
- ☐ Lipstick
- ☐ Peppermint
- ☐ Fur
- ☐ Blush
- ☐ Bow
- ☐ Ranger
- ☐ Resurrection
- ☐ Wave
- ☐ Songbird
- ☐ Needle
- ☐ Yowl
- ☐ Tourniquet
- ☐ Cherry
- ☐ Drone
- ☐ Kite
- ☐ Conscious
- ☐ Cuff
- ☐ Drum
- ☐ Remote
- ☐ Intricate
- ☐ Willow
- ☐ Crescent
- ☐ Ominous
- ☐ Coalescent
- ☐ Prayer
- ☐ Frozen
- ☐ Bay
- ☐ Worm
- ☐ Power
- ☐ Soul
- ☐ Luminescent
- ☐ Hornet
- ☐ Hue
- ☐ Zealous
- ☐ Ink
- ☐ Imp
- ☐ Wish
- ☐ Mermaid
- ☐ Rome
- ☐ Straw
- ☐ Window

- ☐ Pumpkin
- ☐ Morale
- ☐ Foil
- ☐ Hymn
- ☐ Coral
- ☐ Hunt
- ☐ Concrete
- ☐ Woven
- ☐ Justice
- ☐ Trope
- ☐ Gargoyle
- ☐ Mutiny
- ☐ Seed
- ☐ Scorched
- ☐ Tail
- ☐ Arch
- ☐ Jagged
- ☐ Jungle
- ☐ Dante
- ☐ Regret
- ☐ Tyranny
- ☐ Empire
- ☐ Instant
- ☐ Jasmine

PROMPTS BY GENRE

Below find all of our prompts, divided by genre. Some prompts fit more than one genre; of course, you are also welcome to change the genre of a given prompt as you see fit.

Action/Adventure

- ☐ Before the existence of post offices and telephone lines, letters and news of importance were entrusted to Messengers.
Write a story about a Messenger who bears the news of an enemy invasion and his desperate run to his nation's capital and King.

- ☐ In a fictional country still ruled by a monarch, a political faction within the government has the King secretly assassinated. They believe the King's son will be easy to control, thus allowing them more power within the country. When the Queen rather than the Prince succeeds the throne, the traitors find they may have bitten more than they can chew.

☐ While pulling off a high-stakes heist at a gangster's home, a thief steals something that was not on the agenda. "Someone," actually.

☐ A blackmailing ring targets a popular singer with a net-worth in the millions of dollars. The job is to be a quick profit: The singer in question is known to be an utter airhead, and the blackmailers expect her to bend at the slightest pressure.
Unfortunately for the criminals, the singer's "dumb-blonde" persona is completely staged. The woman beneath the make-up and outrageous outfits is in fact quite shrewd - as well as very, very vindictive.

☐ A murder mystery leaves a small-town police force baffled. The police Chief contacts the federal government for assistance. What he gets is a tiny, messy, psychotic woman with an FBI badge and the title of the best investigator the agency's ever seen.

☐ A heist gone wrong, a death, and honor among thieves.

☐ A retired superhero is forced to pick up the mantle once again when her children are threatened.

- ☐ Two young children - a boy and a girl - are out trick-or-treating with their parents for the first time. At a particularly well-decorated house, an automated witch scares the little boy into crying. His sister promptly takes action.

- ☐ A schoolgirl hires an out-of-work detective to find a lost necklace that had been given to her by her mother.
  He finds it, along with a whole lot of trouble.

- ☐ A man fresh out of college decides to go backpacking across Europe.
  A day into the journey, he realizes that his idea of what travelling abroad entails differs greatly from the reality.

- ☐ A thief steals a cursed statue. As his luck takes a turn for the worst, he tries to return the statue.
  The previous owner proves to be a problem.

- ☐ A man heavily in debt to a shady underground organization attempts to escape gangsters and corrupt cops as he tries to figure out a way to return the money - and keep his life.

- ☐ A girl falls through a crack in time into a dimension identical to ours, with the exception of it not being inhabited by living beings.

- ☐ A girl is dragged into an adventure quite against her will.

- ☐ Historically, astronomers were often employed by the ruling nobility. They read the stars in order to foretell coming events of importance, such as wars, draughts, or famines. Write a story that features such an astronomer, and a forthcoming disaster.

- ☐ After a shipwreck, a man finds himself stranded on a remote and unpopulated island. What's worse, the only other survivor of the wreck appears to be his ex-wife.

- ☐ True strength is in the mind. Write a story in which a strong man is pitted against a smart man, and loses.

- ☐ In a world on the verge of destruction, a scientist accidentally discovers time travel.

- ☐ Apollo, the Greek god of music, truth, and prophecy, falls in love with a human promised to the god of war, Ares.

- ☐ A spirit attaches itself to a woman and wrecks havoc in her life. After a consultation with a medium, the woman learns that the only way to get rid of the specter is to find the person responsible for its death and bring them to justice.

- ☐ Two soldiers of opposing armies experience a surreal time of truce when a terrible earthquake collapses part of the battlefield, trapping the men in an underground cavern.

- ☐ An ailing King chooses to give his kingdom to his youngest son, bypassing his elder brother. The scorned son is enraged and hatches a plan to kill his brother and gain the crown.

- ☐ A renowned secret agent is tasked with stealing an important document from the home of a Mafia Don. During the operation, he runs into another man set on the very same document – a thief with a flamboyant personality and a flair for the dramatic that grates on the agent's nerves. When the two men are discovered by the Don's security, they have to work together in order to avoid being captured.

Fantasy/Sci-Fi

- [ ] A star falls in a family's backyard. Only it's not a star but a very friendly alien.

- [ ] Your pet dragon is misbehaving.

- [ ] The shadows on your wall are speaking. Write about the conversation that follows.

- [ ] A magical mishap shrinks your character for twenty four hours. How does the day go?

- [ ] A girl grows wings. Nothing else about her changes, and no explanation seems forthcoming about where the wings came from. What is more, they seem to have a mind of their own...

- [ ] Your character has been turned into a magical creature. What kind of creature is it? How does their day go?

- [ ] An ordinary, boring man gains a superpower. What kind of power is it? What does he do with it?

- [ ] An angel and a demon are trapped in a single mortal body after a supernatural mishap. What happens?

- ☐ Write a conversation between a dragon and the princess it has captured.

- ☐ A little girl brings her pet demon to show-and-tell at school.

- ☐ A little boy tells his imaginary friend what he wants to be when he grows up.

- ☐ A mermaid gossiping with a cat.

- ☐ A geneticist successfully creates a talking dog. Now, if he could only get the stupid thing to shut up...

- ☐ A boy gets sucked into his favorite video game. Write a short scene around a single level of that game.

- ☐ A scientist observing a meteor shower sees something other than stars falling to Earth...

- ☐ Write of a world in which wishes come true - if one is willing to pay their price.

- ☐ A woman buys a dog from a local shelter, for company. The dog turns out to be a wolf. The wolf ends up turning into a person.

- ☐ A girl trades her smile for material wealth.

- [ ] A historical figure is resurrected, and sent to spend a single day at a modern-day high school/college. What do they think? Need inspiration? Resurrect one of the following:
  - Julius Caesar
  - Cleopatra
  - Vladimir Lenin
  - Aristotle
  - Friedrich Nietzsche

- [ ] A little girl makes a silly wish on a four-leafed clover. It comes true.
- [ ] A boy visits the moon with his best friend (who is also an alien).

- [ ] A thief steals something precious from the Garden of the Sun. What is it? Does he/she manage to get away?

- [ ] Imagine that there was in fact a place where the world ends. What would it look like?

- [ ] A woman finds a genie in a bottle.

- [ ] An army of Teddy Bears protects a young child from monsters.

- [ ] A pumpkin turns into a handsome young man on Halloween Eve.

- [ ] A girl talks to her shadow.

- [ ] Her shadow talks back.

- [ ] A man is star-struck. Literally. And an alien princess is really, really sorry.

- [ ] A girl drops through time and space, and ends up in a strange world where cat-like, humanoid creatures are the ruling race.

- [ ] A goddess turns into a mortal woman and walks the Earth.

- [ ] A poor man meets his Luck.

- [ ] A man has the Devil's own luck. Literally.

- [ ] Aliens have lived on Earth for thousands of years. Some hide themselves from humans; others walk among them in disguise. A man and a woman are trapped inside a burning building. One of them is of an alien race; in order to save both of their lives, he/she needs to betray his/her secret.

☐ Superstitions are a common thread in many cultures. Describe a world in which superstitions are true, and then place a character whose luck works backwards in that world.

For example: A black cat crossing one's path leads to bad luck in this universe; however, when that happens to your character, he/she wins the lottery.

Here are some common superstitions:
- **Breaking a mirror:** Seven years of bad luck (usually when it comes to love)
- **Walking beneath a ladder:** Bad luck
- **Saying goodbye on a bridge**: You will never see the person you said goodbye to again
- **Opening an umbrella inside:** Brings bad luck
- **Right hand itching:** You will be giving money soon
- **Left hand itching:** You will be receiving money soon.
- **Spilling salt:** Bad luck, unless a pinch of it is thrown over one's right shoulder

- It's the year 2304. Intergalactic flight has become a possibility, with new discoveries and advances made all the time. A young scientist signs up for a routine exploratory mission. His/her team is to visit a planet near Earth that has been found to sustain plant life. The scientist in question is very unassuming and shy - easily overlooked by the rest of the crew and senior members of the science department.
  Which is probably why he/she gets left behind on the strange planet.
  With its very strange inhabitants.
  Who turn out not to be limited to plants.

- While on vacation with her parents, a teenage girl finds a strange, gem-colored stone in the sea. She takes it home with her.

- A woman in middle age is thrown back in time, into her teenage body.

- A fair princess loses her beauty to a curse. It's the best thing that has ever happened to her.

- A little girl gets lost in a field of sunflowers. A kind scarecrow shows her the way home.

- [ ] In Japan, it is believed that if one folds a thousand paper cranes, their most desired wish will be granted.
  A girl folds a crane every day, for a thousand days. She makes her wish as she folds the wings of the thousandth crane.

- [ ] Strange things happen when a witch sneezes.

- [ ] A woman moves into an apartment rumored to be haunted. Turns out it is. The woman and the resident ghost end up making pretty great roommates.

- [ ] An alien ship accidentally abducts a man as it passes over his house.

- [ ] A superhero and a super villain are best friends in their daily lives. Neither is aware of the other's secret identity.

- [ ] A small, dense forest is rumored to be the meeting place of strange, dark things. One full-moon night, two teenage boys decide to find out if the rumors are true.

- [ ] A day in the life of a misanthropic telepath.

- [ ] A race of humans believed to have gone extinct some time before the birth of the first homo-sapien is discovered still very much alive and well at a secluded and previously unknown island. A team composed of scientists and military personnel is sent in to make contact.

- [ ] Imagine dinosaurs were actually dragons, and that folk lore related to the fire-breathing beasts is true. Write a story of an ancient civilization's interaction with the giant lizards.

- [ ] A woman's "third eye" opens. Literally, and in the middle of her forehead.

- [ ] A day in the life of a misanthropic telepath.

- [ ] A vampire bemoans the shameful way in which his race is being depicted in contemporary pop-culture.

- [ ] A woman is robbed of her dream of becoming an actress when she is attacked and disfigured by what she believes to have been a rabid dog.
  The following full moon, she realizes something else altogether has happened to her.

- ☐ A sailor goes overboard during a terrible storm. He loses consciousness, only to wake up surrounded by strange people on an unknown island. The man does not understand the language the people speak, and the people have never heard of the man's native land.

- ☐ A wizard accidentally turns his wife into a crow. He kind of wishes she had taken a different form. Something without a beak would have been much preferred.

- ☐ A character gains the ability to turn invisible. What is the first thing they do with it?

- ☐ An airplane pilot sees something extraordinary in the sky.

- ☐ The boogeyman discusses the hardships of his job in a late-night show interview.

- ☐ Baba Yaga is a well-known character in Russian folklore. Usually described as an old, powerful sorceress living in a hut balanced upon a single chicken-leg, Baba Yaga is a mercurial being: At times cruel, at times benevolent.
  Write a story about a child who stumbles upon Baba Yaga's hut.

- [ ] A woman finds a beautiful golden necklace. Rubies and diamonds weave along it - as do strange runes that feel warm to the touch.

- [ ] A statue comes to life.

- [ ] A witch is seeking an assistant. Pay negotiable, hours flexible. May involve activities of dubious legality.

- [ ] A hunter spots a large red fox. After several hours of tracking and careful herding, he corners the beast.
  Only to watch it transform into a beautiful woman.

- [ ] In many cultures, it is believed that a person's name holds power over the person themselves. Write a story about a woman who has lost her name.

- [ ] A rich man loses everything - his wife, his home, his job, most of his savings - in the span of a couple of months. He is convinced that he is cursed, and goes to a famous esoteric for help.
  By the end of the session, the man has annoyed the person running it so badly that if he weren't cursed before, he sure is now.

- [ ] Something magical happens on a lazy, rain-drenched afternoon.

- [ ] A girl finds a hand-written poem tucked between the pages of a book on Advanced Biology she borrows from the school's library. She reads it out-loud, charmed by the silly rhymes.
  It turns out the poem is not a poem, but a spell.

- [ ] A man stumbles upon a garden in full bloom. Atop a mountain. In the middle of winter.

- [ ] A boy suddenly grows bunny ears. High school gets a lot more embarrassing.

- [ ] A man who fears heights gains the ability to fly.

- [ ] The temperature in one of the rooms in a certain family's home is always drastically different than that of the rest of the house. The family often jokes that the room must contain a door to a different dimension. Turns out, they are right.

- [ ] A woman suffers from terrible nightmares. Her dreams turn out to be prophetic.

- [ ] A little boy slips and falls from a bridge into a deep lake.
  He is saved by a kind, if a bit strange creature.

- ☐ A man grows up hearing rumors about a strange woman living alone deep in the forests of a nearby mountain. Some call her a witch; others dismiss her as unsound of mind. The man decides to find out if the woman exists and if so, if the stories about her hold any truth.

- ☐ Two tiny faeries sneak into a child's bedroom, meaning to spirit her away.
  The child's pet poodle is having none of it.

- ☐ In Greek mythology, there exist beings by the name of "Furies:" terrifying female demigods who take vengeance upon mortals guilty of terrible crimes.
  Write about a man haunted by a Fury.

- ☐ Every year on her birthday, a girl obsessed with fantasy books wishes for something magical to happen to her.
  On her twenty-first birthday, her wish finally comes true.

- ☐ A man grows horns. And then a tail. Wings, too.
  He really wishes that people would stop screaming and pointing.

- [ ] An evil wizard is transformed into a kitten, courtesy of a failed spell meant to bring doom to his enemies.
  Ignorant of what had happened, one of said enemies decides to take the wizard-turned-kitten for her pet.

- [ ] Unrest in their native lands forces an alien princess and her family to emigrate to Earth. The girl is about fifteen Earth years old, and not too thrilled about attending a human school.
  Especially since no one on Earth even knows of her planet's existence.

- [ ] After pissing off the wrong person, a man is transfigured into a woman for one month. In other words, he is literally forced to walk into someone else's shoes.

- [ ] A boy wakes up to see flickering lights by his bedroom window.

- [ ] Early morning by the sea. An old fisherman sits on a deserted beach, patching up a long coil of fishing nets.
  Suddenly, a figure emerges from the sea. It walks up to the fisherman and sits beside him.

- [ ] In German lore, there exists a "Christmas demon" by the name of Krampus. On Christmas Eve, Krampus accompanies Father Christmas and punishes the children who have been bad, while St. Nicholas leaves gifts for those who have been good. Krampus is commonly depicted as carrying a bundle of birch sticks, rattling long chains, and generally looking very devil-like.
  Write a story about a boy who has misbehaved during the year, and thus encounters Krampus on Christmas Eve.

- [ ] Describe a world of magic.

- [ ] At a party, a woman kisses a frog someone found on a dare.
  It turns into a prince.

- [ ] A girl introduces her father to her imaginary friend.
  Said friend is not exactly imaginary.

- [ ] A troll visits a human village.

- [ ] A girl visits the future. It is nothing she would have ever expected.

- [ ] A demon complains to an angel about his job.

- [ ] A strange flower has bloomed in a neighborhood garden. Its petals are pitch-black, its leaves large and blue-green, and its aroma has people seeing bizarre things indeed.

- [ ] Hans Christian Andersen's beautiful fairy-tale, "The Snow Queen," begins with the breaking of the Devil's mirror - a large, ghastly thing that twists whatever is reflected in it to appear ugly and wrong. Pieces of the mirror are carried all over the world, entering people's eyes and bodies and wrapping their perceptions of reality. Write a story of someone who has inadvertently swallowed a piece of the Devil's mirror.

- [ ] A girl meets an online friend for the first time. Only they turn out to be...not exactly human.

- [ ] A man finds the end of the rainbow. What is on the other side?

- [ ] A girl meets a dust fairy that lives beneath her bed.

- [ ] Personify the days of the week. Write a story that has them interacting with each other.

- [ ] A girl fights off a very real monster with nothing but kindness.

- [ ] A boy becomes an adult in the span of a day.

- ☐ A girl discovers she has a fairy-godmother. A very quirky, possibly insane fairy-godmother.

- ☐ A man finds a strange music box that plays different tunes depending on the mood of the person who opens it.

- ☐ A little girl believes that her next-door neighbor is a wizard. Despite what her parents think, she is not actually wrong.

- ☐ Following his parents' death, a young boy finds himself bumped from relative to relative, with no stable home or loving care to be found. After a year of such misfortune, he is suddenly adopted by a mysterious uncle he had never previously met. The man is rich and extremely kind to the boy. He is also a bit magic.

General

- [ ] A teenager is visiting his grandmother in her small hometown village. Describe a day they spend together.

- [ ] A man sees a boy snatch a woman's handbag. He chases after the thief and is able to catch up to him - only to find out that the boy is his son.

- [ ] A teacher finds a letter written by one of the worst troublemakers in her class. The letter is addressed to the boy's mother, and seems to have been discarded, unsent. What is in the letter?

- [ ] Two travelers sit beneath a large, old tree and talk about the places they have seen during their wanderings.

- [ ] The tree from the previous prompt grumbles about humans while it listens to the travelers' conversation.

- [ ] A girl chases after baby ducks in her grandmother's backyard.

- [ ] A girl protects her little sister from bullies.

- [ ] A young mother saying goodbye to her child on his/her first day at school.

- ☐ Three friends pool their money together and buy a whole bunch of lottery tickets. One of the tickets ends up winning half a million dollars! What do they do with the money?

- ☐ A woman is invited to the engagement party of a friend who, years earlier, got her fired in order to take her job. The friend does not know that the woman is aware of his/her betrayal.

- ☐ An old woman discovers the fountain of youth. If she drinks from its waters, she will be young and beautiful again - but will also forget everything she has ever experienced. What does she do?

- ☐ A boy buys a gift for his mother.

- ☐ Three siblings reunite after the death of their father.

- ☐ A happy puppy playing with its favorite human.

- ☐ First day at an out-of-state college for a girl who has never been away from home.

- ☐ A man walks up to his boss and quits his job of twenty years. Describe the scene.

- ☐ A woman thinks over her marriage as she signs papers requesting a divorce.

- ☐ Changing schools is never easy. Especially if the transition is from a private school to a barely-funded public high school. The son of a certain disgraced politician is about to find that out first hand.

- ☐ An old man throws a coin in a wishing fountain. What does he wish for?

- ☐ A woman returns to the city in which she grew up after many years away.

- ☐ A man catches his sixteen-year-old daughter smoking. He himself is a smoker. What does he do?

- ☐ A little boy takes care of his mother while she has the flu.

- ☐ A boy eavesdrops on a conversation between his parents, and learns something surprising.

- ☐ A man helps his granddaughter learn how to ride a bike.

- ☐ A bandit finds a lost little girl by the side of a deserted road.

- ☐ A boy shares his sandwich with a stray dog. The dog follows him home.

- ☐ A girl moves to a new school. The school in question has a terrible bullying problem, especially among girls. Newcomers in particular are eaten alive.
  This newcomer, however, is not someone bullies should mess with. As they are about to find out.

- ☐ A boy gets sent to the principal's office for fighting. While waiting to be seen, he meets a girl that is there for a similar reason.

- ☐ An accident robs a woman of her beauty. How does she face the world, after?

- ☐ A little girl wants a puppy. After months of begging, her parents finally cave in; they take her to the local dog shelter and let her pick one of the many puppies romping around.

- ☐ The little girl falls in love with a big, scary Doberman instead.

- ☐ A musician tries to leave his management company, only to discover that the company has cheated him out of most of his earnings.

- ☐ A bratty teen is convicted of a minor crime. As the teen in question is a repeated and unapologetic offender, the judge sentences him/her to a week in actual prison as a lesson.

- [ ] A shy boy makes a friend on his first day in kindergarten.

- [ ] A man lives off scamming women for their money and possessions. He is an expert at emotional manipulation, and has not had so much as a single criminal charge raised against him.
  His latest victim, however, proves tougher to crack than the rest. Possibly because she is a detective who has been tailing him for the past several months.
  Not that her scamming beau is aware of the fact.

- [ ] A little girl gets into her mother's expensive make-up.

- [ ] An overworked secretary finally snaps and gives her boss a piece of her mind.

- [ ] A woman who has not worked a day in her life finds herself joining the blue-collar workforce when her husband suddenly dies and leaves her facing bankruptcy.

- [ ] A brilliant woman who works in a meaningless, low-paid job finally gets her lucky break.

- [ ] A man is let go from his job when his company downsizes. He is unable to find another job in his profession, so he has to temporarily settle for a menial position. Too embarrassed to tell his family, the man pretends he still works at his old office when he is in fact flipping burgers at a local fast-food place.

- [ ] A day at the Aquarium turns hilariously chaotic when a giant octopus escapes its tank.

- [ ] A woman overly-concerned with other people's opinions is dreadfully embarrassed of her carefree sister. Said sister could not care less.

- [ ] A college professor is reading through an essay exam most of his students failed. Describe several amusingly terrible responses, and the professor's reaction to them.

- [ ] A woman quits her job and starts her own knitting business online.

- [ ] A college grad is looking for a job and has, in growing desperation, applied to everything from burger joints to corporate offices. Describe several interviews he/she goes to. Try to make them as comically awful as possible.

- [ ] A foreign exchange student is trying to get used to the local culture. His/her host family is ridiculously enthusiastic about helping him/her do so. They are also very ignorant of the student's own culture, and bombard him/her with well-meant but often strange questions.

- [ ] A busy, overworked father imagines what his life would have been like, had he not gotten married.

- [ ] Mothers have the (at times, annoying) habit of being right. Write a story in which a mother has the cause to say "I told you so" to her willful child.

- [ ] A boy happy with life on his family's farm is sent to a boarding school in a far-away city.

- [ ] A boy from a poor family makes it into one of the most exclusive schools in his country. He is there on a scholarship, and everyone else is very aware of the fact.

- [ ] A man witnesses a father viciously castigating his son. The boy flinches constantly, hinting at further abuse.
  The man steps in.

- [ ] A woman meets her husband's lover.

- ☐ A woman finds out the company she has worked in for over thirty years plans to let her go.

- ☐ A down-on-his-luck man is sitting on a bus stop, waiting for a bus that is to take him to yet another job interview. An older man sits beside him. After several minutes, the older man begins to talk: He questions the young man about his troubles and gives him advice. The advice in question seems strange to the younger man, but he decides to follow it.
  His life changes around almost immediately.

- ☐ A grocery store clerk helps a lost little boy find his mother.

- ☐ A group of college friends meet again after ten years apart. Life has changed a lot for all of them, but it has not changed them or their friendship.

- ☐ A woman decides to give her unborn child up for adoption.

- ☐ A woman leaves law-school in order to pursue her dream of becoming a pastry-chef. She is a terrible cook, but it all works out anyway.

- [ ] Greed tears two brothers apart when they discover a chest filled with gold buried in their late-father's back yard.

- [ ] A train accident leaves a close-minded businessman stranded in a small, developing nation.

- [ ] An Army veteran visits a monument built to commemorate the soldiers who have fallen in a certain war. The names carved in the stone are ones the man knows well.

- [ ] An aging actress takes an embarrassing role in the hopes of recapturing her previous fame.

- [ ] Two kids playing on the beach discover a strange little creature.

- [ ] A basketball coach watches on in despair as the few students who have come to basketball try-outs attempt to outdo one another in clumsiness.

- [ ] At a high-end store, a snobby sales representative insults person after person. He is especially vicious toward a bookish-looking woman, not realizing that she is the daughter of the store's owner.

- ☐ A little boy builds a fort out of his grandfather's prized book collection. The grandfather is torn between tears and laughter.

- ☐ A little boy finds a lizard while playing in the park and puts it in his mother's purse. The mother gets a surprise while looking for her wallet in the grocery store.

- ☐ Two whiny kids meet their new babysitter: A small, sweet-looking lady. The kids take bets on how long it will take to make her cry. They are in for a big surprise.

- ☐ A set of identical twins completely opposite in character decide to switch places with each other for a day.

- ☐ There are many wonderful teachers out there. And then there are those who go to work only to get their paycheck.
  Write a story featuring a bad teacher and a class bored out of their minds.

- ☐ A girl/boy from a small, homogenous town moves to a metropolis filled with people from all over the world.

- ☐ An old man reminiscences about his youth while watching his grandson at play.

- [ ] A man whose father was a gambler visits a casino. Describe his reaction to the people inside, the atmosphere, and the memories of his father the casino brings back.

- [ ] A psychologist is psychoanalyzed by one of his patients. The psychologist is not amused.

- [ ] After months of silent suffering, a man tells off his mean, inconsiderate, and very muscled coworker.
  Said coworker promptly breaks down into tears.

- [ ] A man says something hurtful to a person dear to him. He regrets it immediately but words, once spoken, cannot be taken back.

- [ ] The members of a popular boy band are forced to split up when several of them file a lawsuit against their management company. Although they are all close friends, part of the band chooses to remain with the company while the rest decide to leave it. Write of the days leading to the decision to file the lawsuit, and its aftermath.

- [ ] An annoying door-to-door salesman tries to harangue his way into a person's home.

- ☐ Two twenty-something intellectual-wannabes are discussing "things of importance" in loud voices while riding on a crowded public train. A woman on her way back from work sits near the duo, trying to ignore them.

- ☐ A grouchy, single, middle-aged man gets saddled with his sister's children over a long weekend.

- ☐ A teen has taken to talking in text-lingo. His/her parents can no longer understand a word he/she is saying.

- ☐ Describe a day in the life of a young woman living in a dangerous neighborhood.

- ☐ A moody teenager goes shopping with her mother.

- ☐ A sales representative at a high-scale cosmetics store is torn between honesty and the desire to make a sale as she watches a customer load her cart with expensive, but absolutely unsuitable make-up products.

- ☐ A boy finds out his mother had been an actress after purchasing an old VHS tape from a local rental store that's going out of business.

- ☐ Unable to find a job after graduating college, a brilliant young man/woman finally succumbs to the need for money and takes a menial job at a local supermarket. He/she expects a boring, if physically demanding days and is not at all prepared for the work-drama that awaits.

- ☐ A man who is direct and honest by nature finds himself in a work environment where slyness and subtle cattiness are the norm in office interactions.

- ☐ A girl finds her mother's old diary.

- ☐ A naturally timid person is put in a situation in which being aggressive is the only way to go.

- ☐ A mechanic with a gift for writing has secretly been submitting his stories to a small magazine for years.
  When one of his stories is nominated for a Pulitzer Prize, the man finds himself scrutinized by the literary world - and found lacking.

- ☐ A landslide leaves a group of hikers stranded in a mountainous region during a terrible storm.

- ☐ A woman falls asleep in her office at work. When she wakes up, she finds that she is alone, the office is dark, and all the doors are locked. Knowing that she has no excuse about missing the punch-out time and not particularly eager to be fired for sleeping on the job, the woman decides to spend the night there instead of calling for help.
She finds quite a bit to occupy her time, especially in the files kept in her boss' office.

- ☐ A woman who no longer believes in anything witnesses a miracle.

- ☐ A little white lie snowballs into a great big problem.

- ☐ A lonely man finds solace in the most unexpected place.

- ☐ A man finds a fox cub in his gardens. It appears sick, so he brings it home and attempts to heal it.

- ☐ A noble is banished to the outskirts of the kingdom after he commits a small transgression at Court. Initially angry at his dismissal from the Capital, the noble soon finds himself warming up to the provincial town he has been tasked to administer.

- [ ] An old woman recounts the greatest triumphs in her life.

- [ ] A teenager overhears his mother complaining about him/her to her best friend. At first, the teen feels angry; then he/she realizes his/her mother is right.

- [ ] A woman loses everything she thought she wanted, only to find herself with everything she actually needs.

- [ ] A warrior thinks about the things that rule his life: Battle, King, and family. He realizes he only cares about one of them.

- [ ] A famous boxer is forced from the ring for the sake of his health. At loose ends and in the possession of too much built-up aggression, he decides to join a knitting club. It proves to be much less relaxing than advertised.

- [ ] A celebrity goes to his/her high school reunion, mostly out of spite. High school was not the best time of his/her life, and he/she is eager to show off a bit.

- [ ] A boy is studying to be a botanist. His father, a retired Army Colonel, is not too pleased.

- ☐ While clearing out her family's basement, a woman finds a picture album that belonged to her grandmother.

- ☐ A man gains perspective after an accident at work leaves him with a temporary loss of sight.

- ☐ A man who has long ago given up on his dreams has his dearest wish literally fall into his lap.

- ☐ A woman lives in a fantasy world of her own making; she immerses herself in books and movies, ignoring or wrapping the reality around her.

- ☐ Two farmers talk about the drought that has befallen their country. One is superstitious, and believes the draught to have a supernatural cause; the other is realistic and points to more logical reasons for the lack of rain.
  As a result, she is quite unprepared to face the real world and its less-than-nice inhabitants once she leaves the safety of college.

- ☐ After a storm destroys their home, a family discovers a treasure buried in the house's foundation.
  Every evil for good, people say.

- [ ] Two little girls break their mother's collection of glass elephants while playing. Their mother sits them down and explains the importance of respecting what other people hold dear.

- [ ] Write a story in which an apparent injustice is explained and given reason.

- [ ] Two kids plan an adorable, loving Mother's Day for their hardworking mom.

- [ ] A woman meets her idol, and finds him lacking.

- [ ] A goat herder teaches a scholar something about life that is not taught in books.

- [ ] A bad cold has a girl losing her voice. Forced to be silent, she learns a lot about her friends and family.

- [ ] A man discovers that a family of foxes has made a home beneath his house.

- [ ] A warrior takes a beautiful sword as spoils of his most recent military success.

  The sword is haunted by the ghost of a man the warrior killed during battle.

Horror

☐ A woman receives a gift from a secret admirer. It arrives in a small crate that is cold to the touch. The accompanying note states that her admirer wishes he could touch her heart with his words.

☐ A surly teenager wakes up in one of the Grimm Brother's more morbid fairy tales: Bluebeard.

☐ A little girl hears a strange noise coming from a dried-up well. She stands on her tippy-toes and peers over the well's rim, and sees…

☐ A strange girl is riding the train late at night. A man approaches her.

☐ Two friends lose their way in the mountains while hiking. Thankfully, they are able to find an empty cabin before night sets around them. It is well-stocked, the heat is running, and all electronics – except the phone lines – seem in check. As the night progresses, however, strange things start to happen…

☐ A toddler draws something strange during playtime at school.

☐ Dark skies, empty world.

- [ ] Strange things come out to play on moonless nights.

- [ ] A thin dirt road winds through a large forest. Local lore is filled with stories about people going missing after following the road in the forest's depths, and the trail itself has come to be referenced to as "the Ghost Path." A young man walks down the Ghost Path on a dare. An hour or so after entering the forest, he loses both the road and his way.

- [ ] A man gets stranded in the middle of nowhere, Romania. He does not speak a word of Romanian, is almost out of cash, and has no idea where he is. He resolves to walk until he hits civilization. The sun has set by the time he reaches a small village...

- [ ] A man meets a strange woman in a dark forest.

- [ ] A King makes a foolish, selfish deal with Fate. His son must bear the consequences.

- [ ] A razor-sharp smile.

- [ ] A man sells his soul to save his life. Is it worth it, in the end?

☐ An actor is chosen as the lead in a movie depicting the life of a brilliant - and quite a bit insane - nineteenth century businessman. The actor has trouble getting into character, so his agent suggests he familiarizes himself with the businessman's history. To do so, the actor travels to his character's native city and spends the weekend at the late-businessman's home, which has been turned into a museum. When the actor returns to the set the following Monday, he performs marvelously. He does not, however, appear to be fully himself - or *only* himself...

☐ While looking through her photo album, a woman notices an unfamiliar man in the background of one of her wedding-day photos. She looks carefully through the rest of her photos and, with growing horror, realizes that the man is in every. Single. One.

☐ A child disappears while playing with a friend in its own backyard. The friend seems terrified and refuses to speak. The local police cannot find a trace of the child, or any indication that the child had at any point left his/her family's property.

- [ ] A man finds the gate to the Underworld. The heavy doors are slightly parted. Curious, the man leans in and tries to see what lies hidden behind them...

- [ ] A girl bullied terribly at school stumbles upon a strange website that promises to solve all of her troubles.

- [ ] The following is believed in cultures across Europe: If you hear your name called out late at night you should not turn around, for it might be the Devil calling you.
  One dark night, a man is alone in his home when he hears someone calling his name. He turns around.

- [ ] An old sinner prays for absolution. At the same time, a pious young man commits a grave crime.

- [ ] Working in a funeral home can get pretty boring. Then there are those days when a corpse comes to life...

- [ ] After her village is razed to the ground on the orders of a greedy and merciless King, a woman makes a deal with the Devil in order to get revenge.

- [ ] A girl is gifted with a beautiful doll. Soon, the girl notices something strange: The doll's hair seems to be getting longer...

- [ ] A man who has the ability to see the future foresees his child's murder. He recognizes the person responsible, as well.

- [ ] A meteor collides with Earth. In addition to the widespread damage and enormous loss of life, clouds of dust have risen in the atmosphere, plunging the planet in darkness. A year after the incident, survivors have somewhat adapted to their new, darker lives. That is when strange beings start to emerge from within the dark skies...

- [ ] A merchant is traveling through a forest on his way to a town in which he plans to sell his wares. He chances upon a small pond; thirsty, he halts his horse and unsaddles. Water-jug in hand, he kneels by the pond. Freezes.

    There is something staring up at him from within the lake's depths.

- [ ] A man falls ill with a strange sickness. He begins to sleep more and more, his dreams grow as vivid as reality, until he can no longer separate reality from fiction.

Humor/Magical Realism

- [ ] Write a WANTED ad for a serial cat burglar who is, in fact, a cat.

- [ ] Let's banish some monsters! Write a funny story featuring your biggest fear.

- [ ] Pick a celebrity and feature them as a character in a story - folktale, myth, whatever you like.

- [ ] Write about a goose whose best friend is a cat.

- [ ] A character finds a magical turtle. It follows him/her around and tries to "help" by making small wishes the character utters aloud come true. The results are more embarrassing than anything else.

- [ ] A character you have created comes to life. Congrats - you've got a new roommate!

- [ ] Write about a lawyer who lives in a city at the bottom of the sea.

- [ ] Write a story featuring a character that is completely clueless about what is happening around them. Recommended genre: Humor.

- [ ] A fox transforms into a human for a day. Write what follows.

- ☐ A dim-witted knight decides to take on a fire-breathing dragon in order to save a lovely princess. The dragon is more amused than anything else.

- ☐ A stressed-out businessman is turned into a cat by one of his clients.

- ☐ A bear moves into a new apartment building and goes to introduce him/herself to the neighbors.

- ☐ Your mobile is judging your text messages.

- ☐ Describe a humorously terrible day of family fun at the beach.

- ☐ A brattish Prince runs away from home. He meets a bored bandit at a small, crowded tavern. What happens?

- ☐ A man gains the ability to speak with inanimate objects. Describe his first day at work following the strange occurrence.

- ☐ Two cockroaches, talking about life.

- ☐ A bunny and a Doberman play together.

- ☐ Two skunks take a walk around their neighborhood.

- [ ] Dionysos, the Greek god of wine and revelry, takes a mortal form in order to visit the human world. Only he might've been one goblet too many into his wine while he was performing the enchantments that turned him into a human. He is now stuck in the body of an elderly woman in downtown New York.

- [ ] A pirate captures the son of a corrupt British noble and blackmails the man for ransom. While the boy's father is properly cowed, the boy is more excited than scared by his being kidnapped by pirates.

- [ ] A demon takes a human form in order to trick a pious mortal into giving away their soul. Only, the mortal in question is not so easily duped: He/she sees through the demon's disguise and baits the demon right back.

- [ ] Misadventures in cooking. Pasta on the ceiling, fire in the oven - that sort of thing.

- [ ] A baby duck imprints on a lawyer, and follows him wherever he goes. Including the courtroom.

- [ ] A cat's guide on being a responsible human-owner.

- ☐ Teleportation has become a reality. Write three funny scenes of teleportation gone wrong.

- ☐ Friends don't let friends get drunk and troll the FBI.

- ☐ Life's not easy when your boss is a spoiled witch.

- ☐ A vampire, an incubus, and a werewolf walk into a bar...

- ☐ A family visits Disney Land for the first time. The parents are more excited than the kids, and the kids just want their parents to *stop embarrassing them already*!

- ☐ No good deed goes unpunished. Especially when the good deed in question is taking in your neighbor's grumpy old cat.

- ☐ A scene from the life of a stressed-out boy-band manager.

- ☐ A woman is trying to learn how to cook. Her boyfriend is trying not to die via food poisoning.

- ☐ A dog is afraid of thunder. So is his owner.

- ☐ A little boy gets lost in the woods. Thankfully, a friendly bear finds him and helps him home.

- ☐ A journalist incidentally kidnaps the son of a famously corrupt CEO.

- ☐ A little boy finds a hedgehog, and decides to bring it to his kindergarten class.

- ☐ A virtuoso musician is hiding a terrible secret: He cannot read a single note of music.

- ☐ Two elderly women sit on a bench and gossip about their neighbors.

- ☐ Grocery shopping in a store with annoyingly helpful employees.

- ☐ The end of the world has come...and it is unlike anything anyone could have ever imagined.
  Write a unique scenario for the end of the world. Bonus points if it is funny.

- ☐ A young, beautiful woman suddenly grows a long, green beard.

- ☐ Meet Hedgehog and Otter, the best detective duo the world has ever seen.

- ☐ Introduce technology into a fairy or folk tale. Example: Red Riding Hood chatting with granny on a Smartphone, the Three Little Piglets rocking it out on DDR...

- A girl's pet snake is uncharacteristically loving, and extremely protective of her owner.

- We all have a "little voice" inside our heads. Yours has escaped the confines of your mind and gained a body.

- A mouse helps a cat find her way back home.

- An actor has finally gotten his big break: He is to play King Arthur in a big Hollywood production.
  Only problem is, he may have bent the truth a bit when it came to the list of skills on his resume. Particularly the one to do with his mastery of horse-riding.

- A stressed-out college senior mistakenly turns in a fanfic he/she wrote in the stead of his/her term paper.

- What is the silliest, most useless thing you have ever purchased? Write a story that features the item in a life-saving role.

- Two idiots accidentally save the world.

- A little boy befriends the monster beneath his bed.

- An old, grandmotherly woman is waiting in line to buy tickets for a heavy-metal concert.

- [ ] A man forgets his cell phone in the park. He realizes his mistake almost immediately, and is able to retrieve the phone before it disappears. When he goes back home, the man notices that there is a voicemail left on his phone. The caller is not someone he recognizes, and the message is begging the man for help in finding someone named...Mittens?

- [ ] Loki, the Norse Trickster God, is a bit peeved at mortals' apparent disregard of his existence. So he does what he does best: He makes trouble.
  Unfortunately for his ego, he manages to get himself caught up in his own mischief.

- [ ] The wives of two brothers cannot stand each other. Write a funny story around a family event, featuring the women's interaction.

- [ ] Write a story about a tiger in a tutu.

- [ ] A little girl dresses up the family's pet cat and has a grand adventure in her grandmother's flower garden.

- [ ] A couple decides to have the husband be the stay-at-home parent, while the wife continues to work.
  The husband quickly comes to regret this decision.

☐ A man and his daughter live in a two-story apartment building. When the family above them moves out, an extremely rude pair of college students rents the place. The two are noisy and inconsiderate, and generally make it impossible for the man to sleep or do his work. After a week of this, the man is furious but still too polite to say anything to the troublemaking duo.
Fortunately, his daughter does not have the same problem.

☐ A witch loses her flying broomstick. A local grandmother tries to sweep cobwebs off her ceiling, and gets quite the surprise.

☐ A small boy chases after a frog, loses his shoe, and ends the day by eating some dirt.

☐ An anniversary dinner turns into a total disaster. Ex-girlfriends, bad meat, faulty appliances, and nosy neighbors all make an appearance.

☐ The world's best secret service agent is a fraud. Not that he/she knows it.
Write about a secret agent who is terrible at his/her job, but has such an amazing luck that his/her missions are always unmitigated successes.

- [ ] A bunny tries to teach a cat how to hop.

- [ ] A preschool teacher on too-few cups of coffee tries to bring a classroom of adorable, mischievous toddlers to order.

- [ ] A duck thinks it is actually an airplane.

- [ ] A family inadvertently adopts a squirrel as a pet.

- [ ] A young married couple purchases their first home. It is an astonishingly beautiful property located in a secluded nook toward the end of a small mountain town. The couple cannot believe their luck in finding the property - and receiving such a wonderful deal on it, to boot! The morning following their first day in their new home, the couple discovers the reason for the house's low price: It is strangely, unfortunately popular with the local wildlife.

- [ ] Write about a super-powered villain whose only weakness is... being hugged.

- [ ] A writer's house keeps getting invaded by a curious kitten.
  The writer is allergic to cats.

- ☐ A lion escapes from the zoo and ends up in the backyard of a local kindergarten. A little girl befriends him.

- ☐ A man is being stalked by a pink elephant that only he can see.

- ☐ A man wakes up in a field, surrounded by curious sheep. He resolves to limit his drinking. That, or get better friends.

- ☐ Two women who do not know each other strike up a conversation on the train. They share stories about their kids, give each other advice, and generally bemoan the hardships of motherhood.
  It is not until the end of the trip that it becomes apparent one of the women had been talking about her pet cats the entire time.

- ☐ A girl gets "discovered" - but not for a talent she would have ever expected.

- ☐ It is 'bring your daughter to work' day. A stressed-out lawyer takes his daughter to his office. She takes her stuffed giraffe along. Everybody has a much better day as a result.

- ☐ A grown man cries over something silly.

- ☐ A cat blackmails its owners for food and cat stuff and general household dominance.

- [ ] A teenage girl is feeling a bit down in the wake of moving to a new school. She goes to the local mall in the hope of cheering herself up. The following happens, in no specific order:
    - The bus she is on breaks down.
    - She loses her phone.
    - A seagull steals her sandwich.
    - She befriends a ninja.

    It is the best day she's had in a long time.

- [ ] A little kid and a bear cub share a jar of honey. Their respective mothers are quite perplexed on what to do.

- [ ] After a night of drinking, a brave warrior faces his biggest challenge yet: His furious wife.

- [ ] A CEO takes up knitting for relaxation. It works, for the most part. Plus, there's the added bonus of instilling fear in his subordinates as they watch him crochet furiously during his lunch breaks.

- [ ] A man and a woman are in a relationship. Both want to end it, but believe the other is still in love and will be hurt. Write a humorous story about their attempts to let each other down easy.

- ☐ A family is sick of rude telemarketers. So they make a game out of confusing and bewildering unwanted callers.
  Describe four such calls, one for each family member.

- ☐ Little Red Riding Hood goes into the forest on her way to visit her grandmother. Only she does not meet the Big Bad Wolf, but the Sassy Red Fox. The two have some great adventures together.

- ☐ Two friends make everything into a competition. Including baking cookies for a tea party that they have both been invited to.

- ☐ Write the hypothetical schedule of a full-time housewife with two children and one forgetful husband.

- ☐ Drunk chickens.

- ☐ A woman buys a pet pig.
  Her long-suffering roommate seriously considers selling it to the local butcher.

- ☐ A woman accidentally pepper-sprays her boss.

- ☐ A camping trip turns surreal when a terrible storm forces a family to take shelter in a cave... and bunk with its furry inhabitants.

- [ ] They say dogs look like their owners. Write a story in which a good-natured Great Dane watches on in confusion as a tiny Pincher barks enthusiastically at him. In the background, the same scene repeats with the dogs' owners.

- [ ] A detective is trying to interview an astonishingly conceited, dense woman in connection to a crime. The woman is convinced the detective is flirting with her.

- [ ] A fancy tea party is ruined by a band of vindictive clowns.

- [ ] Being a doctor is difficult.
  Being the nurse assisting a grouchy doctor is even more-so.

- [ ] A sweet woman turns grouchy when sick. Her boyfriend is not prepared for the transformation.

- [ ] Write a short story about a day in the life of a Flight Agent. Flight delays, rude customers, and lazy co-workers abound!

- [ ] A toddler teaches his/her stressed-out parent that being messy is okay, sometimes. Kind of fun, too!

- [ ] A duck waddles into a library.

- ☐ Write a story in which a wife has reason to call her husband "idiot" at least four times.

- ☐ A girl forgets her phone at home. Her mother "accidentally" goes through her messages. Long story short, a certain secret boyfriend is invited to (interrogation) dinner.

- ☐ Two mothers drink coffee in one of the women's living rooms. Their two young children are playing nearby. The mothers are discussing their children.
Several feet away, their children are discussing the mothers.

- ☐ Three not-so-bright individuals discuss world happenings over beer.

- ☐ Two sisters, five and seven each, attempt to bake cookies while their mother takes a nap. An oil-soaked carpet, a ceiling sticky with cookie-dough, and a visit from the fire department later the mother swears off naps - and possibly cookies - for the foreseeable future.

- ☐ A silly wolf plays with a little girl in a park while her mother reads a trashy romance on a nearby bench.

- ☐ A dog saves its owner from the evil, loud, things-sucking machine (aka: the vacuum).

- ☐ Quitting smoking is not easy. Grumpiness is not the worst possible side effect of nicotine withdrawal, but it is definitely in the running. Especially when one is at their annoying boss' house for dinner.

- ☐ A pizza boy has his weirdest house visit yet.

- ☐ A bulldog is not the most reliable security system.

- ☐ A young boy sees snow for the first time. He thinks it is cotton and jumps right in the biggest pile of snow he can find.

- ☐ A superstar gets spotted by fans while trying to do some grocery shopping. He narrowly escapes being mobbed by adoring fans and ends up hiding in a back storage room with an employee who may or may not be high.

- ☐ A sleepy news-anchor completely botches a story on live TV, with hilarious results.

- ☐ A family is looking for a new couch. Cue slick salesmen and unimaginably ugly divans.

- ☐ An exasperated editor is haranguing a famous but lazy author for a final draft of his latest book. Which was due about a week ago.

- ☐ Write a story that includes the following: Two owls hooting on a roof, one pre-finals college student trying to sleep, and a bemused police officer answering a call about a crazy person throwing shoes at birds whilst screaming in Latin.

- ☐ An author is mortified when a trashy book he/she wrote for some quick cash tops the NY Times Bestseller's List.

- ☐ A man attempts to take care of his wife while she is sick with the flu. He mostly fails.

- ☐ A cat napping on a sun-drenched windowsill wonders why her owners are always so grumpy. Don't they have a nice place to nap?

- ☐ A man grows a beard. His wife is not thrilled.

- ☐ A cat and a dog are transformed into humans. Their owner is most bemused.

- ☐ A pathological liar weaves an intricate - and quite fictional - story for a group of naive admirers at a party. His best friend watches on with a mixture of amusement and exasperation.

- ☐ A large, orange tomcat plays while his owner attempts to study for her nursing exams.

- ☐ A mother of two feels like a single parent to three unruly kids when her husband joins in on the whining.

- ☐ A little girl finds a frog in her locker at school.

- ☐ A little boy drinks his mother's cup of coffee while she is not paying attention.

- ☐ Cool-kid wannabe's grandmother friends him on his social media account.

- ☐ A family moves into a house infested with...bunnies?

- ☐ A drunk man stumbling home late at night wonders if he is seeing things, or if there really is a cat sporting a top-hat lounging on his front steps.

- ☐ Two housewives with neighboring houses have a passive-aggressive battle involving baked goods, yard sales, and increasingly extravagant home decorations.

- ☐ Two lions lounge atop the warm rocks in their cramped zoo enclosure, planning on how to get to the annoying people waving and shouting at them but feet away.

- A poet is forced to take a job writing songs for pop-stars at an entertainment company. He submits quality work, but more often than not has his lyrics revised or completely rejected. In a fit of anger, the poet writes a song filled with the corniest, most trite lines he can think of.
It is an unimagined success.

- A rooster meets a vegetarian fox.

- A little girl grooms her pet dog. The poor dog finds itself sporting a feathered hat, clip-on earrings, and curling rolls in its fur.

- What is meant to be a relaxing day out fishing turns hilariously disastrous as a group of children stumble upon a man's fishing spot and proceed to bug both him and the local wildlife.

- Two sets of grandparents fight over the name of their newborn grandchild. Each wants the baby named after someone in their family. Tired and exasperated, the baby's mother names her child after her favorite book character and tells everyone to get out.

- [ ] A man buys an owl and trains it to carry letters.
  People really, really hate getting mail from him.

- [ ] Working the night-shift has turned a woman nocturnal: She sleeps during the day and stays up all night, regardless of whether it is a work day or the weekend. The change of lifestyle does not bother the woman too much. Her neighbor, on the other hand, is convinced she has become a vampire.

- [ ] An extremely clumsy man accidentally stops a would-be robbery by tripping over the bad guy.

- [ ] A girl's father is really enthusiastic about technology, despite being absolutely dreadful at using it. He buys the newest smart-phone available on the market, and then proceeds to bug his daughter with questions.

- [ ] A girl writes a fanfiction featuring her favorite actor.
  Said actor reads it and comments about the story on live TV.

- ☐ A set of fraternal twins, a boy and a girl, look and act astonishingly alike. So much so that their friends at times make embarrassing mistakes...

- ☐ A timid girl finds herself caught between her two best friends when they have a falling out. Driven to the end of her patience, she gives them both a piece of her mind - and scares them right back into a friendship.

- ☐ Write a story set in the Wild West. Feature a cowboy who cannot shoot a gun and a woman meant to be a love interest who cannot care less about romance.

- ☐ Write about a birthday celebration that involves bad presents, exploding cake, and accidental intoxication.

- ☐ A girl makes an embarrassing music video as a joke. Her little brother posts it online without her knowledge.
  By the next morning, she is internet-famous.

Journaling

- [ ] Have you had a reoccurring dream? What was it about? Write a short story around it.

- [ ] Create a holiday! Describe its history, how to celebrate it, etc. Word it as an essay about the holiday - as if completing a boring school assignment.

- [ ] Write an origin story for the Easter Bunny.

- [ ] Describe a place you find beautiful and calming. It can be imaginary or real.

- [ ] Create a deity. Describe its origin, its powers, how it looks - anything you want.

- [ ] Create a creature. Describe how it looks, where it lives, what it eats, its behavior.

- [ ] Make up a word. Give the definition and use it in a sentence.

- [ ] Write about a trip you have taken. If you have ever traveled outside your native country, write about that journey: What stuck with you?

- [ ] Write about a world that has no colors in it.

- ☐ Create and describe an alien planet capable of sustaining life. How closely do you imagine it would resemble ours? What kind of life would it bear?

- ☐ Write a short story from the perspective of a fairy-tale villain. For example, the witch from *Hansel and Gretel*, or the Queen from *Snow White*.

- ☐ Write a story featuring one of your ancestors.

- ☐ Describe a rainy evening in a busy city.

- ☐ Make yourself a cup of coffee or tea. Now, foretell your own future by reading the patterns in the liquid.

- ☐ Pick a name, at random. Research its history and write a short summary of its roots.

- ☐ Write a short story featuring a British sailor exploring the oceans in the 1800s.

- ☐ Write about a tragedy that does not feature death or blood: A simple, everyday heartbreak.

- ☐ Write a story about a young girl whose family has recently emigrated from their native country to the United States. The girl does not speak English, and none of her classmates speak her language.

- [ ] The Hammurabi Code dates back to Ancient Mesopotamia (1754 BC), and is one of the oldest codes of conduct ever deciphered. Its laws encompassed all aspects of Mesopotamian society, and the punishments for transgressions were very harsh.
  If you had to create a Code of Conduct that would govern a society, what would it look like? What laws/punishments would it feature?

- [ ] Write a story that takes place in a society in which the color of one's eyes determines one's social class.

- [ ] Describe a universe that is the exact inverse of our own, in whatever capacity you choose.

- [ ] You become a character in your favorite book.

- [ ] What is the most embarrassing thing that has ever happened to you? Write a story around it.

- [ ] Imagine that an important historical event never happened. What would the world be like today, if that were the case?

- [ ] Write a story based on the following line: "Love is blind, deaf, and very, very sarcastic."

- [ ] Describe an ordinary, everyday miracle.

- ☐ They say that people who grew up near the sea or ocean cannot happily live inland. Tell the story of a woman who returns to her hometown by the sea after years spent away.

- ☐ Write about a personal triumph. Why was it important to you? What made it special?

- ☐ Write a story featuring a germophobe in a European country where cheek-kissing is the normal means of greeting.

- ☐ List five things that you like to do, and why.

- ☐ A father teaches his sixteen-year-old daughter to drive. It's pretty much a disaster.

- ☐ A runaway kitten wrecks havoc during a domestic flight.

- ☐ Where would you live, if you could choose? Why?
  It can be a real or a fictitious place.

- ☐ "There is good to be found in every evil." Write a story in which the above holds true.

- ☐ "Whatever you do, you do it to yourself." In other words: Write a karma story!

- ☐ Write a story inspired by the following line: "The revolution is in your mind."

- ☐ Think of a time someone said something especially stupid or insulting to you. Write a story in which you respond to that person in the manner you wished to at that time, but likely did not.

- ☐ Standing by a friend during a difficult time in their lives is glorified by society. But what if doing so is harmful for the person doing the "standing?"
  Write a story in which a person breaks contact with a friend in need in order to save their own sanity and nerves.

- ☐ Have you done something that you later regretted? What was it? Looking back on the situation now, do you believe you could have - or should have - acted in a different way?

- ☐ Check today's horoscope for a zodiac sign of your choice. Write a story around a character of that sign who has a day exactly as foretold by his/her horoscope.

- ☐ Evaluate the following saying:
  There is no good without evil, and no evil without good.

- ☐ If you could relive a day in your past, which day would it be? Why?

- [ ] Do you have a pet-peeve? What is it? How do you deal with it, when you encounter it?
- [ ] Tell a story about a cloud.
- [ ] Has something made you disillusioned with the world, however briefly?
- [ ] Write about an absolutely lazy day, where nothing of note happens but everything is wonderful anyway.
- [ ] Write a story of a self-made man. Make sure to include his views on the world and his fellow people.
- [ ] Create a Coat of Arms for your family, including a family slogan to go along with it.
- [ ] Write of a world where everything exists in extremes. There is nothing uncertain and nothing in-between; everything is either one way or another. Evil is evil, good is good, love is fanatical and hate - all-encompassing.
- [ ] Write a story of betrayal.

Mystery/Thriller

- [ ] An elderly woman is gardening when she discovers what appears to be a treasure map buried in her back yard. It seems to lead to a spot on the outskirts of town. What does she find where X marks the spot?

- [ ] A young man is in a minor accident. When he wakes up in the hospital following the incident, he sees a strange being sitting by his bed. Who/what is it? What happens?

- [ ] A girl sits on a bridge, singing. She seems sad. Who is she? Write a story about her.

- [ ] A writer meets a mysterious woman in a bar. He feels drawn to her; what is more, she seems strangely familiar...

- [ ] A man purchases a strange pet in a mysterious pet store.

- [ ] A teenage boy helps his aged neighbor clean her house as she prepares to move out. Touched, the woman tells him that he is welcome to anything he finds in the attic. What does the boy find?

- ☐ A man works for a delivery service in a remote, mountainous area. One morning, he receives a suspicious-looking crate to deliver to a local farm.

- ☐ A woman receives a strange phone call. The caller's voice is muffled and somewhat difficult to understand. What does the caller want? What does your character do?

- ☐ A young girl gets lost while camping with her class. She stumbles upon a strange hut in the forest…

- ☐ A dark night in a foreign city. A tourist is walking along the banks of a river, on her way back to her hotel. Suddenly, a shadow shifts to her right. She turns--

- ☐ Two strangers meet on a dark road in the middle of a forest. One has a secret; the other is running from something.

- ☐ A man is driving towards work, in heavy traffic. Suddenly, the car next to his disappears. So does the one in front of him, the one behind him…until he is quite alone on the road.

- ☐ A man finds a strange ring in his wife's purse.

A Year of Creative Writing Prompts

- ☐ Two friends are on a road trip when they are caught in a terrible storm. Their car is wrecked, their phones are out of service…and they seem to have ended up somewhere strange indeed.

- ☐ A mysterious store sells strange perfumes.

- ☐ A boy finds out his father is a pod-person.

- ☐ A teenager hacks into a government database and sees something he definitely should not have.

- ☐ A man finds a strange door in his basement. He cannot recall ever seeing that door before…

- ☐ A new drug has been invented. It makes people happy, energetic, optimistic. Almost everyone takes it.

    Write about someone who does not use the drug, but is surrounded by people who do.

- ☐ A woman lives high in the mountains, far away from other people and civilization in general. One winter night, in the midst of a blizzard, a knock sounds on her door.

Love in Ink

☐ A naive man is scammed into buying a worthless property situated in the middle of a gloomy swamp. Having spent most of his life savings, he has no choice but to move there.

☐ A detective tries to untangle a strange case: A woman has been kidnapped the night before her wedding. The groom does not seem to be too worried; neither do the woman's parents.

☐ A man is playing with his dog in the park. He throws a Frisbee for the dog to chase, but when the dog comes back, it is not the Frisbee that it holds clenched between its teeth.

☐ A traveler meets a kindred spirit on the road. However, as their journey progresses, strange things begin to happen - and they all seem to center around the man's new companion.

☐ While battling a fire, a firefighter becomes trapped in a burning room. A young boy finds him just before the ceiling collapses and leads him to safety.
After being released from the hospital, the firefighter seeks out the family who owned the burned house in order to thank the boy. The family, an elderly couple, receives him warmly - and with some confusion.
They do not have a son.

- [ ] A string of bank robberies leaves the local police baffled. No matter how fast they are or how many security cameras the given bank has, the thieves are never seen or caught. An inside job begins to seem more and more likely.

- [ ] A door-to-door salesman becomes a witness to a crime.

- [ ] A week lost at sea has a sailor losing his mind.

- [ ] Write a story based on the following anecdote:

  A man was on his way back home. It was getting late, so he decided to take a shortcut through a nearby graveyard. As he walked, he could not help glancing around, a bit spooked by his surroundings.

  After a short while, he caught up with a woman walking along the same path. He relaxed somewhat, happy not to be alone. The woman noticed and gave him a knowing smile.

  "Don't be embarrassed," she said, "I used to be scared of graveyards too, when I was alive."

- [ ] A beautiful golden urn is unearthed at the outskirts of a small Eastern European town. It is a gorgeous, valuable artifact left from an ancient civilization.
It is also not empty.

- [ ] An amateur photographer accidentally takes a photo of a corrupt cop making a deal with a local gangster.

- [ ] A man falls asleep beneath a cherry tree heavy with fruit. Night has already fallen when he wakes up. He makes to get up - and hears strange, hissing voices above him.

The man looks up, and sees...

- [ ] The personal assistant of an important politician notices something strange about some of his boss' financial supporters.

- [ ] A hiker encounters a terrible winter storm while high up on a mountain. Disorientated and unable to make contact with anyone on the ground, he takes cover in a shallow cave to wait the storm out.
Someone else has done the same thing, and the hiker is surprised to find he is not alone on the mountain.

- [ ] There is a strange little house at the end of a quiet suburban street. It's fences are tall, its sides overgrown with ivy and weeds, and the brown paint of its window-ledges has chipped and faded all over. No one ever goes in or out, and the mailman never stops by its rusted mailbox.
  Yet, there is always a light on behind one of the dust-heavy second-floor windows.

- [ ] A woman suffering from severe agoraphobia (fear of situations and places that may cause unpleasantness, often resulting in fear of the outside world as a whole) has not left her home in over ten years. One day, she sees an unfamiliar van parked in front of her neighbor's home. The neighbor's two children are playing outside. The driver of the van beckons them over. The children go closer to the van.
  Realizing what is happening, the woman finds herself in a nerve-wrecking situation and only minutes to overcome her terror of the world beyond her doorstep.

- [ ] A Healer is asked to visit a small village in which a strange sickness wrecks havoc.

- [ ] Two ships pass by one another on a dark, moonless night. The captain of one of the ships hails the other.
No one responds.

- [ ] Only two people come to a man's funeral. One of them is his mother. The other, when asked, says: "I am only here to make sure he's really dead."

- [ ] A young woman inherits an enormous mansion from her great-great-aunt, along with the rest of the deceased's considerable earthly possessions. The only stipulation to receiving the fortune is that the young woman make the mansion her home. The woman is more than happy to comply.
That is of course before she actually sees her creepy new home.

- [ ] A man is awoken in the middle of the night by the mad barking of his neighbor's dog. Disoriented and grumpy, the man opens his bedroom window with the full intent of screaming himself hoarse at the stupid mutt.
His breath catches in his throat when he sees at what the dog is barking.

- A man finds a strange box buried beneath a pile of clothing and shoes in his wife's closet. The box is locked; a note taped to its side reads: "If you open the box, I'm divorcing you."

- A garbage man discovers something strange at a residential dumpster.

- A girl selling flowers on a bridge has a strange customer one late September afternoon.

- A man buys a used car and finds something strange in the trunk.

- A girl encounters a wolf on her way back from a nearby river.

- A priest is sent to minister over a small town on the outskirts of a large kingdom. When he arrives, the priest discovers that the townsfolk continue to adhere to a number of pagan beliefs and rituals. One of them in particular strikes him as strange - and quite a bit disquieting.

- On a hot, sleepless night, a woman wakes up to the smell of something burning and rustling beneath her bed.

- A nice, silly dog turns vicious whenever its owner's boyfriend is around.

- [ ] A man-made virus has been accidentally released, leading to the total annihilation of 95% of the world's human population. The survivors are scattered across the globe, and find themselves no longer completely human.

- [ ] While on a tour of a Victorian-era home, a man falls through a painting into a secret room.

- [ ] A terrible accident leaves a man missing some of his memories. The memory-loss seems limited to a point far in the past, so the man mostly goes on with his life.

    That is until a teenage girl shows up at his house, claiming that she is his daughter. The man has no recollection of the girl or the woman she says is her mother.

- [ ] While walking back home, a young girl is approached by an old woman. The woman can barely walk, and she asks for the young girl's assistance in getting back to her home a block down the street. The girl is a bit apprehensive, but helps the woman nonetheless.

    Everything is fine, until they reach the old woman's house.

- [ ] A couple wins an all-expenses paid trip to an exotic island. The place is gorgeous, the accommodations - extravagant, and the couple falls in love with it all right away. Until night falls and the man-eating creatures native to the island emerge, that is.

- [ ] In a slowly dying world, a young man cares for his ailing friend. The two are the last remaining survivors of the human race.

- [ ] A woman receives a strange package. It is entirely black and has no label or a return address.
  She opens it.

- [ ] Two sisters spend their summer vacation at their grandmother's house. Soon, they notice something strange: There is always a light on in the attic at night, even though their grandmother never goes up there.
  They decide to investigate.

- [ ] A girl dreams a dream she has had many times: A nightmare about a vicious dog that had once belonged to her neighbors. This time, something is different - there is someone else in the dream with her.

- ☐ A man forgets his son at the supermarket. He remembers half-way home and drives frantically back, only to find-

- ☐ A sleep-over turns strange when people begin to disappear... only to return, not seeming like themselves.

- ☐ A girl in white counts crows upon a frozen field.

- ☐ A man forgets his suitcase on the train while traveling home from work. Thankfully, he remembers it in time and is able to hail the conductor and retrieve it.
  When he gets back home, the man realizes he must have the wrong suitcase, as his was definitely not filled with neat stacks of money.

- ☐ The night of the first day of the new year, an anthropologist witnesses a strange dance performed by a group of people in the center of a rural village. Curious, she asks the villagers about the dance and whether it holds any cultural significance.
  The villagers have no idea what she is talking about; no one has left their home the previous night.

- [ ] One afternoon, a woman returns home to find her husband gone - along with all of his possessions. Heartbroken, she assumes that he has left her.
   Five years later, she discovers something that has her rethinking the whole accident.

- [ ] A hot summer day in a small, boring town. A teen is smoking behind a school. Suddenly-

- [ ] A man fixes up his grandfather's old typewriter. Eager to try writing on it, he loads the typewriter with a new sheet of paper; however, a phone call distracts him and he forgets all about it.
   The following day, the man goes back to the typewriter. All is as he has left it - with the exception of the sheet of paper, which is filled from top to bottom with neatly-typed words.

- [ ] A man finds a letter by his front door. It is addressed to him, but bears no stamp or a return address. He opens it. The very first word gives him pause; it reads, "Dad." The man has no children.

- [ ] A visiting opera gains fame when one of its actors dies on stage, during a live performance. What is more, the cause of death is by no means natural.

- [ ] A woman plays a game of chance against the Devil.

- [ ] A sinner walks into a place of worship late at night.

- [ ] After work, a woman boards the train she usually takes home. Her car is almost empty, which strikes her a bit strange - it is six o'clock in the afternoon, well into rush hour. She shrugs it off to luck and sets to reading her book.

  When the train makes its first stop, however, the woman realizes something is wrong. The stop is not one she is familiar with - or indeed, that should exist in reality at all.

Romance/Relationships

- [ ] A love confession letter gets delivered to the wrong address. The sender realizes what has happened and tries to get it back. What happens?

- [ ] A couple bickers over something stupid. The two give each other the silent treatment, then make up. Write the scene.

- [ ] Two men are vying for the attention of a woman. What does each offer? How do they approach her? Who – if either – does she choose in the end?

- [ ] A shy florist falls in love with the owner of the small bakery next door. Unable to say what he feels, he tries to show his feelings through the language of flowers. Unfortunately, his one true love cannot tell a weed from a peony...

- [ ] A chase that spans continents, between two people who profess to hate each other, but cannot quite let go.

- [ ] Two musicians from competing bands fall in love. Each dedicates a song to the other. Their bandmates are not amused.

- [ ] An unlikely romance.

- [ ] A warrior returns home after a terrible war.

- [ ] A girl has reoccurring dreams about a kind boy with a bright smile. Years later, she meets a man who reminds her of that boy...

- [ ] A newly-retired army Colonel visits someone he once loved dearly, but had to disregard in order to fulfill his duty to his country.

- [ ] A man has fallen in love with his best friend. The friend in question has no idea.

- [ ] Two dogs conspire to get their owners together.

- [ ] A couple has recently started living together. They are deeply in love with each other...but not with each other's idiosyncrasies, which the new living arrangement brings to light.

- [ ] Two sisters fall in love with the same man.

- [ ] A super-awkward, truly adorable first date.

- [ ] A man travels across the globe to meet a woman he has only talked to online.

- [ ] A blind date between two people who have in fact met before and hate each other's guts.

- [ ] Two friends complain to each other about their respective significant others. By the end of their conversation, they realize they are talking about the same person.

- [ ] A Viking befriends a young hermit. Write of an adventure the two have together.

- [ ] A man who cannot stand sweets falls in love with a baker. He goes by his crush's bakery every morning, and is inevitably forced to buy - and then consume - something sweet to gain their attention.

- [ ] A computer geek falls in love with a technology-challenged tech-support client.

- [ ] A rock star falls hard for a woman he meets at a charity function. It turns out that the woman is a visiting diplomat from a foreign nation.

- [ ] In a universe where people have soulmates, a man finds his in a most inopportune moment. Namely, at a party at his superior's house, in the form of his boss' wife.

- [ ] A picnic at midnight.

- [ ] In a society where men are traditionally seen as the weaker gender, a young man is getting ready for his wedding day.

- ☐ Two strangers escape a sudden downpour in the same tiny cafe. The coffee is bad, the service is worse; the two still fall in love.

- ☐ Write a story of star-crossed lovers, with an unexpected and unorthodox twist at the end.

- ☐ A man tries to buy his wife an anniversary present that she will, for once, actually like. "Tries" being the keyword.

- ☐ A man attempts to be "cool" in front of his son's friends. The results are embarrassingly humorous.

- ☐ A monk falls in love with a woman he chances upon while collecting apples in the monastery's orchard. He begins to seriously reconsider his vows.
  There is, however, more to that woman than first meets the eye.

- ☐ In the wake of a tragedy, a man decides that it is better to not have a heart than to have it broken.

- ☐ Two powerful families arrange for their children to wed. The future groom and bride meet a week before their wedding.
  It is hate at first sight.

- [ ] A woman goes to a tarot-cards reader in hopes of receiving advice for her love life. The woman she usually goes to is absent; in her place is a stunningly handsome man.

  The woman forgets all about her romance woes.

- [ ] A divorced couple juggles their kids, bills, and their own messy feelings.

- [ ] A man discovers a photograph of a beautiful girl tucked in one of his old textbooks. A name is scrawled on the back of the aged photo. Unable to recall neither the girl nor why he has her picture, the man decides to look her up.

- [ ] A supermodel falls in love with her shy, geeky agent.

- [ ] Write a break-up story. No crying, no hysterics - just a soft, quiet melancholy.

- [ ] There is only one thing to do when your spendthrift son ends up moving back home for the fifth time: Find him a wife. The candidates for the position - all friends or ex-girlfriends of the man - are less than impressed.

- [ ] Instead of performing the song that had been assigned to him, a boy sings something he had created for the girl he secretly likes during a school assembly.

- [ ] Meeting a girl's parents for the first time is always nerve-wrecking. When said parents are a decorated Army General and a Special Ops agent, it is a heart-stopping experience.
  Possibly literally.

- [ ] After losing her job, a woman goes out drinking with friends. She wakes up in someone's bed, hung-over and very much married - to what turns out to be her ex-boss.

- [ ] A woman breaks her arm, loses her job, and is almost evicted from her apartment. Then she runs into a handsome stranger at her doctor's office. Her life does a one-eighty.

- [ ] Growing up in a small town is not easy. There's gossip, drama, constant intrigue over the silliest of things, and if you even think about liking someone...
  Well, it's safe to say the whole town will know within hours, your crush included.

- ☐ In some cultures, it is believed that an even number of flowers is only offered at funerals. A man not aware of this belief gifts his foreign girlfriend with a dozen roses.

- ☐ Without her morning coffee, a woman is an almost literal zombie. One morning, said woman is running late and does not have time for her much-needed shot of caffeine. Which is why she says yes when her boyfriend of two weeks asks her to marry him.

- ☐ A noble in the French Court under Louis XIV falls in love with one of the King's mistresses.

- ☐ A girl gets to meet her biggest idol. It's unfortunate that it happens during the most embarrassing moment in her life.

- ☐ During an office party, a section manager introduces his wife. His subordinates cannot believe their eyes; what is a beautiful, gregarious woman doing with their grumpy boss?

- ☐ Write a short story of an accidental meeting between two people who used to once be in love.

- ☐ A girl kisses a boy on a dare.

- ☐ A brilliant but socially-inept boy attempts to ask his crush out on a date. After some painful mumbling and fidgeting, she takes pity and kisses him.

- ☐ Third time's the charm!
  Or so hopes Mr. Wilson, about to be married for the third time in as many years.

- ☐ A couple who can no longer stand each other go to a marriage counselor.

- ☐ A comedian goes on a blind date. The date is really, really awkward; it does not help that he cannot seem to stop himself from making terrible jokes.

- ☐ A boy does something really stupid to impress a girl he likes. He ends up with a broken arm, but hey - at least she noticed him!

- ☐ Two good friends compete against each other for the affections of the same girl. Said girl does not particularly like either of them.

- ☐ A man buys the bulldog he has always wanted while his wife is away on a business trip. And a cat. And a parrot.

- [ ] Long hours and an unforgiving profession has caused a man to drift away from his family. When he realizes he has not spoken a single word to his children in over a week, the man decides he has had enough and quits his job.

- [ ] A naive, romantic man finds himself charmed beyond reason by a sarcastic, pessimistic woman.
  Let the courting commence!

- [ ] A pair of high school sweethearts grows up and grows apart.

- [ ] A merciless, sardonic, and generally unpleasant man finds himself the romantic interest of a peppy high school teacher who recently moved in next door.

- [ ] A girl confesses her love to a boy, only to have her feelings thrown in her face. Ten years later, the man said boy has become finds himself unknowingly pursuing that same girl.

- [ ] In a world where people are born with the date of their death written on their bodies, a woman falls in love with a man that has a year and a day left to live.

Love in Ink

- ☐ A teenage boy writes awful poems dedicated to his crush. He never meant for her to find out about them, though.

- ☐ A man loses the love of his life, before he ever has a chance to tell her know how he feels.
  A chance encounter with a magical creature gives him an unexpected second chance.

- ☐ A boy discovers that a single smile is at times enough to make one's day better.

- ☐ A man frustrated with his marriage signs up for a dating site. He feels drawn to a woman he meets there, and starts developing feelings for her. The woman, as it turns out, is far from a stranger.

- ☐ A delivery girl is sent to deliver a pizza to the house of her crush. Initially embarrassed, she decides to suck it up and do her job. She is not at all prepared for the awkward, starstruck way in which her crush reacts upon seeing her at his door.

- ☐ A man and a woman marry against their respective families' wishes. Consequently, no one turns up for their wedding. The couple finds it hard to care, happy as they are.

Writing Challenges

- [ ] Write from the perspective of a mouse in a cupboard.

- [ ] Personify an object around you. Your teacup for example. What does it do and say?

- [ ] Describe your morning routine using the most eccentric words and phrases that come to mind.

- [ ] Write a one-scene play about a Princess who has been turned into a Prince.

- [ ] What did you have for lunch? Describe it as if you are in a commercial selling that particular food.

- [ ] Write a short story featuring a minor character from one of your larger works - someone you never had a reason or occasion to flesh out. Make the story about them!

- [ ] An artist is harangued by a woman who wants to buy one of his portraits. Write their conversation. Try to make the story dialogue-only and still convey its plot and characters.

- ☐ Write a prayer. The tone does not need to be religious. Try for a simple, honest wording.

- ☐ Make up a fairy tale. Make sure it has all the fairy tale elements (the adage in particular), but otherwise write as you will!

- ☐ Describe a tree in full bloom. Try not to use cliché phrases.

- ☐ Pick a word/phrase in a foreign language (at random, if you can!) and use it in a story.
  Need some help? Here is a list of ten random foreign words:

  - 朝 **(Asa)** - Morning
  - **До свидания (Dosvi'dania)** - Goodbye
  - **(der) Schatten** - (the) Shadow
  - ανατολή ηλίου **(anatolíilíou)** - Sunrise
  - **Tiarna** - Lord
  - **Guanti** - Gloves
  - **Grasker** - Pumpkin
  - 내기 **(Naegi)** - Miser
  - **Õhtu** - Night, evening
  - **Anioł** - Angel

☐ Set a story in a mythical location, either fictional or historical.

In need of inspiration? Here is a list of ten places of myths, both fictional and not.

- **Alexandria**: City named after Alexander the Great. It was host to a tremendous library (Library of Alexandria) and served as a center of knowledge. The Library's eventual destruction resulted in an immense loss of knowledge still mourned today.

- **Babylon**: A historically important city in ancient Mesopotamia. Known for the wonder of the Hanging Gardens, as well as a setting to a number of Biblical (the Tower of Bibel) and Mesopotamian myths.

- **Elysian Fields**: A mythological realm of final rest for fallen warriors and worthy souls in Greek mythology.

- **Kyöpelinvuori**: A fictional place in the mountains in Finnish mythology. Said to be haunted by dead women.

- **Lemuria**: An ancient land rumored to have been the home of an extremely advanced civilization. Thought to have sunk in the wake of a natural disaster. Thought to have existed between the Indian and Pacific Oceans.

- **Muspelheim**: A realm of fire in Norse mythology.
- **Shambhala**: According to Tibetan Buddhist mythology: An ancient kingdom hidden in the Himalayas, ruled by the governing deity of our world.
- **Troy**: A city in Greek mythology that was besieged and eventually overran by Greek armies. Thought to have been located on the shores of present-day Israel.
- **Valhalla**: In Norse mythology, Valhalla is a majestic hall in which Odin rules over all worlds.

☐ Pick a scene from a movie you like. Now rewrite that scene as a parody.

☐ An old man sits in a garden, alone. Describe his thoughts and surroundings. Try to create a specific mood with your description.

☐ Find a picture you have taken that means something to you. Write a story around it.

☐ Write a story that features characters, but uses no personal pronouns.

☐ Write the world's most dreadfully clichéd poem.

Retell a folktale. Try to include as many different points of view as there are characters in it.

In need of inspiration? Try one the following tales:

- Red Riding Hood
- Hensel and Gretel
- The Big Bad Wolf and the Three Piglets

☐ Write a short story containing an incredible amount of adjectives. Seriously, go wild.

☐ Describe the following words in the most unique way possible:

Love, Desire, Grief

☐ Write a story around a recipe.

☐ Write about something that has happened to you. Style the essay as a newspaper report.

☐ Describe a lazy afternoon. Focus on the mood of the story: Choose words that instill tranquility and comfort in the reader.

- [ ] Set a story in a historic era of your choice. Need inspiration? Try:
    - Ancient Egypt
    - Heian Period Japan
    - Germany, in the years leading up to the Second World War
    - Tsarist Russia, right before the Bolshevik Revolution

- [ ] Write a story centered around a sports game. A soccer meet, a football championship, a basketball practice - whatever you wish, as long as it is the focus of the story.

- [ ] Write a disjointed, chaotic story in which nothing makes sense.

- [ ] Write a love song. Three couplets, as straightforward and honest as you can make it.

- [ ] Draw something random.

    ....Done?
    Whatever you have drawn is the main character in your story, and humanity's only hope against an invasion of evil faeries!

- [ ] A Prince decides that he wants to be a villain rather than a hero. Write the story as a play.

- ☐ Grab a book. Open it randomly and write down the third word in the first full sentence on the page (excluding conjunctures and the like). Do this three times.
  Write a story featuring the three words in a single sentence.

- ☐ Write a single story from three different perspectives.

- ☐ Write a story whose focus is not on the main action, but on surrounding happenings. For example: A robbery is occurring at a grocery store, but the story centers on a woman crossing a nearby street and touches only peripherally on the crime happening a block down.

- ☐ Write a story about a character of a cultural background with which you are not familiar.

- ☐ Write a story in which both a character's outward dialogue as well as inner monologue is recorded. For example, what does a girl on a date with a not-so-suave boy think while talking with said boy?

- ☐ Write a story composed of ten "snapshots" from a person's life, from childhood to old age.

- [ ] Write a story that begins with a noise. Example: BAM! BANG! THUMP!

- [ ] Write a clichéd love story with an unexpected ending.

- [ ] Personify a nation of your choosing. Give it a body, personality, and a name.

- [ ] Write a short story that rhymes.

- [ ] Write a story that contains the following words: "the scent of roses in the air."

- [ ] Write a story from the perspective of a criminal.

- [ ] Fill the following prompt in a genre you have never previously written in:
  While visiting her grandmother, a girl stumbles into a room she does not remember ever seeing before. The room itself seems empty, with the exception of a large, frameless mirror hung on the back wall.

- [ ] Open your fridge. Note down the first five things you see in there.
  Write a story that features all five.

- [ ] Pick a character you have previously written about. Create an outfit for them and describe it in detail.

- [ ] Write a haiku!

    Traditional haiku: A poem composed of 17 syllables, divided in three lines of 5-7-5

    Traditional haiku themes: Buddhism, nature, the seasons, love

    Example, by a famous haiku poet:

    From time to time
    The clouds give rest
    To the moon-beholders.
    -Matsuo Bashō

- [ ] Write a story that has these three elements, in order: Fall, cold, love.

- [ ] Come up with a short monologue that can be performed by a stand-up comedian.

- [ ] A woman receives a late-night visitor in a small, provincial town.
    Write the story from two perspectives: First, from that of the woman's gossipy neighbor who sees the strange visitor knock at the woman's door. Then, from the woman's own perspective.

- [ ] Write a story in fifty words.

☐ Create a character. Give them a name, personality, physical description, and a backstory.

You can structure your description as follows:

Name:
Physical appearance
   Hair color:
   Skin color:
   Eye color:
   Height:
   Weight/body shape:
   Tattoos/other:
Personality
   Strengths:
   Weaknesses:
   Things they hate:
   Things they love:
   Governing principles/morals:
   Goals/motivation:
Background
   Home country and city:
   Family circumstances:

☐ Write a story that has a sudden twist at the end. Something unexpected, yet logical within the confines of the story.

☐ Look around yourself. Describe the room you are in, in as great detail as possible.

- ☐ Write about a single day from the perspective of a dog.

- ☐ Write a story about your childhood home. The story can be based on a real memory, or completely fictional. Try to include as many details about the house and its surroundings as possible.

- ☐ Write a story inspired by the following sentence:
  "Drowning on earth."

- ☐ Write a story that takes place in the waiting are of a train station.

- ☐ Create a summary for a book you want to write.

- ☐ A child receives a phone call from his/her deployed parent. Write their conversation, dialogue-only.

- ☐ Write a haunted house story from the perspective of the ghosts.

- ☐ Describe a place of rest and peace - such as a church, a forest, or a garden - late at night. Toe the line between calm and creepy with your description.

- [ ] Do you speak another language? If you do, write a story in which at least part of the conversation is in that language.
  If you do not, choose a language you have studied - or always wanted to study - and try to include as many coherent sentences in it as you can in your story.

- [ ] The night before their wedding, a young couple receives much-unwanted marriage advice.
  Write the story in three parts: The first should focus on the young bride and her mother. The second should feature the young man and his father. The third describes the wedding.

- [ ] Write a story from the perspective of an individual who is disturbingly obsessed with someone.

- [ ] Gulliver's Travels by Jonathan Swift is, among other things, a tremendously creative and imaginative work. If you were to write a similar book of travel and discovery, where would you send your characters? What would you have them discover?
  Write a scene, or otherwise compose a list of fictional places, peoples, and fauna you would include in such a story.

- ☐ A woman leaves her husband and children, leaving behind only a letter to explain her decision.
  Write that letter.

- ☐ A girl hears colors in sound - be it music, people's voices, or the rustling of leaves. Write a story about how she perceives the world and its inhabitants.

- ☐ Write a story about a person running a marathon in a way that properly conveys the experience of running long-distance. Make the text exhausting - either to read (long sentences, etc.) or in terms of adjectives and description.

- ☐ The following is a real question found on an application for entrance to a Master's degree program in a prestigious U.S. University. Answer it.

  > "Describe an event or experience in which you exercised a significant decision-making, management, or leadership role." (750 word limit)

- ☐ Describe a day filled with fireworks, good food, and laughter - all of life's best things.

- ☐ Write a story that features a stereotypical character, in whatever capacity you wish. Make him/her adhere to all the clichés about his/her "kind," until the very end of the story where he/she acts completely out of character.

- ☐ Make a list of ten books that have been influential in your life.

- ☐ The Chinese Almanac is means of telling auspicious and inauspicious days, hours, and directions of travel. It was widely used in both feudal Japan and China, and is still popular with esoteric healers.
  Tell a story in which the Hour of the Ox (the time between 1 am and 3 am) is featured. If you would like the story to be more accurate, check the site below for the day's Almanac and whether the Hour of the Ox happens to be auspicious or not.

  ***Full link*:**
  http://www.dragon-gate.com/tool/almanac/

- ☐ A fight breaks out in a bar. Describe the scene. Try to create a sense of fast-paced violence.

- [ ] Write a story inspired by this nursery rhyme:

    Monday's child is fair of face;
    Tuesday's child is full of grace;
    Wednesday's child is full of woe;
    Thursday's child has far to go;
    Friday's child is loving and giving;
    Saturday's child works hard for a living.
    But the child that is born on the Sabbath day
    is fair and wise, good and gay.

- [ ] Write a story that includes the following exclamation: "Watch out for the monkey!"
- [ ] Have you ever had to memorize a poem for school? If so, try to recall as much of it as you can. Use the lines you remember in a story. If not, write a story featuring a poem that holds personal meaning for you.

- [ ] James Joyce's incredibly complex novel, Ulysses, is based upon the premises of Homer's The Odyssey in that it depicts the journey of a man to his home.
  Write a story that is, at its heart, one of journeying "back home" - in whatever capacity you choose.

☐ Describe a winter festival, fictitious or real. Try to capture the excitement of the event and the warmth of peoples enjoyment. Juxtapose it with the coldness of the season.

☐ Pick a character from a story you have previously written. Switch their gender. Write a new story featuring that character in his or her new body.

☐ Write ten disjointed sentences.
...
Done? Now include all of them in the same story.

☐ J.R.R. Tolkien will forever be remembered for the wondrous worlds and characters he created. Among Tolkien's many literary accomplishments is the creation of several languages, all with their own linguistic roots and grammar.
Create an alphabet for a fictional language. Name the language and ascribe it to a race of peoples or creatures.

☐ People don't change; they just become more themselves with time. Write a story that explores this saying.

☐ In a long line at the Post Office, with only one clerk working in the front

- ☐ The passage of time depends on one's perception.
  Write about a single day from two different perspectives: That of a fruit fly and of a turtle.

- ☐ Write a cheesy graduation speech filled with clichés.

- ☐ *Die Toteninsel*, or "Isle of the Dead," is a famous painting by artist Arnold Böcklin (1827-1901). The painting was immensely popular with its Central European public, and continues to be of symbolic importance in contemporary film and literature. A copy of a version of the paining is found below. Write a story based on or inspired by this painting.

- ☐ Make up a riddle!

- [ ] Write a story of colors. No matter what you choose as your subject, focus on the colors in the story. Make them the most vivid part of your writing.

- [ ] Write a story in two time periods: One in the present, one in the past, featuring the same characters at different points in their lives.

- [ ] Describe a precious childhood memory. Write with as much detail as you can.

- [ ] Write a story about a character incapable of feeling romantic love.

- [ ] Pick two characters from your previous works; the more dissimilar in nature, the better. Put them in the following situations and describe their reactions.

- [ ] At a birthday party of a person they do not particularly like

- [ ] During an accidental meeting with their secret crush

- [ ] Find an old story of yours - the older, the better. Edit and/or rewrite it. Has your writing style changed with time? How drastically?

- ☐ Time-capsule challenge! Write down five things that you would like to have accomplished in the next five years on a loose sheet of paper. Fold the paper and put it into a glass jar or bottle. Bury it in your backyard (or somewhere you can access in the future).

- ☐ Write a story about wrapped perceptions: A character (or a group of characters, or an entire society) sees something one way, when the reality is completely different.

- ☐ Re-imagine the ending of a fairy tale. What if one of Cinderella's sisters had married the Prince? How about if Snow White had not been spared by the Huntsman?

- ☐ It has been proposed that people's fear of death is partially motivated by our fear of the unknown.
  Write of a world where everyone knows what happens after a person dies. How is death regarded in this world?

- ☐ Write a story that reads like a dream: Convoluted, vivid, seemingly logical yet saying nothing at all in the end.

- ☐

- [ ] In Heian period Japan, women scorned or wronged by their lovers would at times take Buddhist vows and retire to a monastery, usually in a mountain and thus far away from civilization. As the vows included an oath of celibacy and the shaving of one's head, swearing to a life as a nun served as the woman's ultimate denouncement of her beau. Write a story about one such woman.

- [ ] Write a story that begins and ends with the same sentence.

- [ ] Write a story that is as concise as possible. Once you have written it, look over the story again and eliminate any words or sentences that are extraneous. Strive for the simplest, most direct tale you can manage.

- [ ] Write a story that begins with its end.

- [ ] Write a how-to guide regarding the proper use of an iron (for ironing clothes). Explain in steps, with as much detail as possible. Assume that a potential reader knows nothing of operating irons - or even what they are!

- [ ] Write a story in which you deliberately ignore grammatical rules. Try to create certain feelings and effects by doing so, rather than simply writing erroneously.

☐ Write a story around a character that fits one of the sixteen personality types described on the website below.

Full link:
http://www.16personalities.com/personality-types.

You are also welcome to Google-search "personality types" and find a site that you like.

☐ Below, you will find three examples of literary devices writers use to enrich their writing. Use each of them in a sentence.
- **_Alliteration_**: the repetition of initial consonant sounds, often in consecutive words. *Ex*: beastly beauty.
- **_Epizeuxis_**: the repetition of a single word, for emphasis. *Ex*: Living in the countryside is dull, dull, dull.
- **_Pleonasm:_** using more words than necessary in order to make a point. *Ex*: I saw it with my own eyes.

☐ Write a story from second-person point of view.

☐ Capture a single moment of extraordinary emotion in a story.

- ☐ Write a story about the same one hour in the day of three people. You will end up with three stories in one, the only connection being the time during which each is occurring.

- ☐ Write a story with an ambiguous end.

- ☐ Record something that has happened to you as a historian would a past event. Try to be as objective as possible.

- ☐ Think of as many synonyms of (or alternatives to) the following words, as they would be used in a story:
  - Say
  - Beautiful
  - Angry
  - Smile

- ☐ Write a story that begins as follows:
  Two people walk along a long, empty road.

- ☐ Write a short story set in a specific historical period. Focus on the setting, the clothing of your characters, and their manner of speaking.

- ☐ Look outside. Select one object - be it a tree, a house, a car, a person - and write a story around them. Describe the object in as great detail as possible, while avoiding clichés.

- [ ] Pick a song at random. Write a story while listening to it. Write only as long as the song lasts - not a word beyond the last second!

- [ ] In literature, a tragic flaw is a trait in the protagonist of a tragedy that eventually causes their ruin.
  Write a story featuring a protagonist who possesses a tragic flaw.

- [ ] Write a story that is told hour-by-hour, with every hour in a single day mentioned.

- [ ] Write a story that centers around numbers.

- [ ] Write a short story by hand, using your non-dominant hand.
  Do you find yourself thinking more before writing?

- [ ] Write a story that includes the sound of rain.

- [ ] Write a story featuring a character who continuously makes bad puns and tawdry jokes.

- [ ] Pick a current news topic and write a newspaper report on it. Style it as a parody.

- [ ] Write a story that will make the reader smile.

Love in Ink

Thank You!

We hope you enjoyed and were inspired by this book!

Do not forget to follow us on FaceBook at *Love in Ink* (www.facebook.com/LoveInkWriters). There, we share writing tips, writing humor, books we love - all the best things!

We would love to read any stories you write based upon these prompts. Send us a link through FaceBook; make a note if you would like for us to share your story with our fans, as well!

From us, to you, with love.

The Love in Ink Team

Made in the USA
San Bernardino, CA
04 February 2019